felt *style*

35 fashionable accessories to create and wear

felt *style*

Chrissie Day

NORTH LIGHT BOOKS

Distributed to the trade and art markets in
North America by North Light Books
An imprint of F + W Publications, Inc.
4700 East Galbraith Road
Cincinnati, OH 45236

ISBN-13: 978 1 58180 899 5
ISBN-10: 1 58180 899 2

First published in the United Kingdom in
2006 by Cico Books
An imprint of Ryland Peters & Small
20–21 Jockey's Fields
London WC1R 4BW

Editor Kate Haxell
Designer Claire Legemah
Photographer Geoff Dann
Stylist Sammie Bell

CONTENTS

Introduction

I cannot remember a time before knitting, a time when yarn did not run through my fingers and feature in my life. I knitted throughout my childhood; I knitted through my teenage years, and through long hours of night duty as a student nurse. I traveled in many countries and my knitting accompanied me, as it did through long, lonely evenings and sad times, and also through happy, happy times and events. I think if my stitches were tears I would have knitted an ocean by now, but equally much of my work is interlaced with golden memories worked into every stitch, binding the garment together

I knitted on through my children's childhoods and then, as an adult, I was introduced to felt making. I enjoyed the challenge of working with the fibers and yarns to produce felt and it was not long before I was knitting projects in increased sizes, simply so I could felt them down to the required final size. Over time I have re-worked and refined my patterns, tested hundreds of different yarns, and this collection is the fruits of those labors—knitting patterns specially designed for felting and step-by-step projects for making wonderful items from wool.

Nature is a constant source of inspiration for me, from glorious vistas and enticing oceans seen on my travels, to my beloved garden. No matter what the season, I always find some inspiration for a new project just by walking out of my back door. I have also collected ideas from architecture that grasps my attention as I travel, whether it be a new prize-winning airport in Madrid, or a peeling painted door in Greece. I love experimenting and adding different fibers into my projects, combining wool with other materials, and using techniques in unusual ways to interpret my ideas and to push the medium of felt further.

Choosing colors, fibers, and yarns from the fantastic array available is always hard and I hope the colors I have chosen in this book inspire you, but do not be afraid to work these designs in your own chosen colorways, or even use different yarns. You can create wonderful, personalized projects with substitute yarns, but remember to check that the fiber content is the same as the yarn specified, or you will not get the same results from the felting process. Turn to Yarn Information on page 124 and check the fiber content of the yarn specified against the one you want to use. Also check the quantity of yarn in your chosen ball against the list as, even if they are a similar yarn and the same weight ball, different brands may contain different amounts of yarn.

Knitting and felting are addictive yet calming, and will help you be at one with the ups and downs of life. Let them into your world and enjoy the journey as much as I have done.

CHRISSIE DAY

1
Bags

Simply stylish bag

This easy knitting pattern makes a perfectly pretty little felted bag that is an ideal gift for a girlfriend, if you can bear to give it away!

YOU WILL NEED

- One 3½ oz (100 g) ball of Adriafil Baba in white/beige (A)
- One 1¾ oz (50 g) ball of Karabella Roses in pale pink (B)
- US 15 (10 mm) 24 in (60 cm) circular needle
- Knitter's sewing needle
- Pair of plastic bag handles
- Sewing needle and thread

TECHNIQUES

- Knitting for felting, page 110.
- Felting knitting in the washing machine, page 111.
- Drying a felted item, page 111.

Finished size approximately 9½ x 9½ in (24 x 24 cm), excluding handles.

Abbreviations page 125.

Variation

Dreamy shades of purple make for a gorgeous evening bag, finished with black circular handles. The yarns used here are:

- One 1¾ oz (50 g) ball of Colinette Point 5 in blue
- One 1¾ oz (50 g) ball of Prism Impressions in mauve/blue/green

To make
Bag

Using both yarns together, loosely cast on 21 sts.
Working back and forth, work 8 rows st st.
Pick up sides

Pick up 10 sts along first row edge, 21 sts along opposite long edge, and 10 sts along second row edge. (62 sts)
Place marker at round end.
Working in the round, knit 49 rounds.
Bind off loosely.

Making up

Weave in any loose ends.

Felting

Following the instructions for Felting Knitting in the Washing Machine, machine-wash the bag to felt it. When the felting process is complete, follow the instructions for Drying a Felted Item,

putting an object of a suitable size (a fabric conditioner bottle, filled with water works well for this project) inside the bag to help shape it while it dries.

Finishing

Using the sewing needle and thread, sew the plastic handles to the inside top edges of the bag (see page 12).

Sea-blue bag

Inspired by the colors of the sea, this bag will hold all you need for a day out—at the beach or in town. Though you have to knit with multiple yarns, the pattern is very simple to follow, so try it.

YOU WILL NEED

- One 1¾ oz (50 g) ball of 4-ply pure wool in each of turquoise and black. Wind these balls together to make one ball of turquoise and black yarn (A)
- One 1¾ oz (50 g) ball of Victoria Smedley yarn in each of gray mohair (B), blue mohair (C), and pink/turquoise mohair (D)
- One 1¾ oz (50 g) ball of Plymouth Spazzini in blue (E)
- One 3½ oz (100 g) hank of Colinette Giotto in green (F)
- US 10½ (7 mm) 32 in (80 cm) circular needle
- US 11 (8 mm) 32 in (80 cm) circular needle
- Knitter's sewing needle
- Magnetic bag fastening
- Pair of plastic bag handles
- Sewing needle and thread

TECHNIQUES

- Knitting for felting, page 110.
- Felting knitting in the washing machine, page 111.
- Drying a felted item, page 111.

Finished size approximately 9½ x 10½ in (24 x 27 cm), excluding handles.

Abbreviations page 125.

To make
Bag

Using US 10½ (7 mm) needle and A, B, C, D, and E, loosely cast on 72 sts. Join ends, being careful not to twist stitches, and place marker at round end. Working in the round, knit 25 rounds. Join in F and knit 5 rounds. As you work, pull F out when knitting some stitches to leave a few loops of yarn on the right side of the work.
Change to US 11 (8 mm) needles.
Break D, E, and F.
Knit 20 rounds in A, B, and C.
Break C and join in D.
Knit 10 rounds in A, B, and D.
Break D and join in C.
Knit 10 rounds in A, B, and C.
Cont in last yarn combination.
Shape top
Next round: [K7, k2tog] rep to end.
Next round and every alt round: Knit.
Next round: [K6, k2tog] rep to end.

Next round: [K5, k2tog] rep to end.
Next round: [K4, k2tog] rep to end.
Next round: Knit.
Bind off loosely.

Making up

Weave in any loose ends. Using the knitter's sewing needle and one strand of turquoise yarn from A, sew up the bottom seam of the bag.

Felting

Following the instructions for Felting Knitting in the Washing Machine, machine-wash the bag to felt it. When the felting process is complete, follow the instructions for Drying a Felted Item, putting an object of a suitable size (a large circular vase works well for this project) inside the bag to help shape it while it dries.

Finishing

Attach one side of the magnetic clasp to the inside center of each top edge of the bag, following the manufacturer's instructions and ensuring that the sides of the clasp are opposite one another. Using the sewing needle and thread, sew the handles to the inside top edges of the bag, as shown below.

Pink flower bag

A fabulous combination of vibrant colors and a blooming flower, embellished with a sprinkling of baroque glass beads, makes this little evening bag into a great style statement. Make your version in colors to complement your favorite party outfit.

YOU WILL NEED

- Towel, bamboo mat, and bubblewrap
- Plastic resist, template on page 123
- Pale pink and fuchsia pink merino fibers
- Sprinkling bottle of warm soapy water
- Piece of fine mesh fabric
- Scissors
- Beading needle and thread
- Magnetic clasp
- Selection of glass baroque and seed beads

TECHNIQUES

- Felting over a resist, page 116.
- Drying a felted item, page 111.

The first layer of pale pink fibers is lying at right-angles to the second layer.

1 Lay the towel then the bamboo mat on the work surface, and place the bubblewrap, bubble-side up, on top of the mat. Lay the plastic resist on top of the bubblewrap. Cover the resist with small sections of pale pink fiber, laying them in one direction across the resist. Add a second layer of fibers, placing them at right-angles to those in the first layer, as shown. Make sure that the fibers overlap the edge of the resist all around and that the plastic is evenly covered.

If you find it tricky to smooth the fringe of fibers over the edge of the resist, try using a piece of wet cloth instead of your fingers.

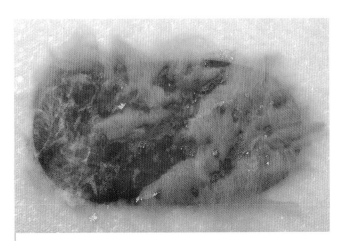

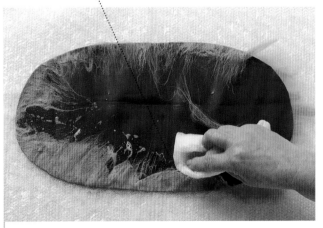

2 Soak the fibers with warm soapy water from the bottle. Lay the mesh fabric over the wet fibers and gently rub over the net to create a lather.

3 Carefully lift the net off the fibers and turn the resist over. Gently flip the fringe of fibers over onto the plastic and smooth them down.

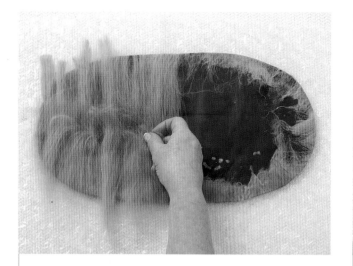

4 Repeat Step 1 to cover the bare side of the resist with a layer of pale pink fibers. Again, make sure that the sections of fiber overlap the edges of the resist all the way around, and that the plastic is evenly covered. Soak the fibers with soapy water, lay the net on top, and create a lather, as before.

5 Repeat Steps 1–4 to cover both sides of the resist with a layer of fuchsia pink fibers, laying them on at right-angles to the upper pale pink layer. Make sure that the fibers overlap the edges of the resist all around. Soak and lather the fibers as before.

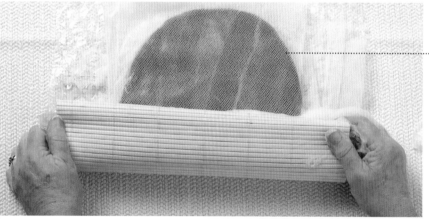

The edges of the fiber-covered resist should be smooth with no protruding strands of fiber.

6 Roll the mat up, with the bubblewrap still inside it. Roll the mat back and forth 50 times to felt the fibers together. Unroll the mat, then roll it up again in the other direction and roll it 50 more times to complete the felting process. Leave to dry.

With the bag cut open it is easy to see how the two different-colored layers of fibers produce a bag that is one color on the inside and another color on the outside.

7 Approximately two-thirds of the way along the felt shape, cut across one layer of felt. Slip the resist out of the felt. Cut the top layer of felt around the smaller end to make the bag flap, as shown. Trim the edges to neaten them.

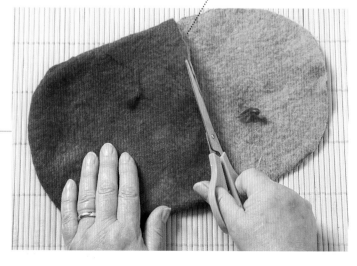

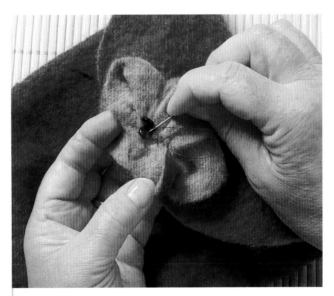

9 Using the beading needle and thread, sew the petals together to form a simple flower shape.

8 Using scissors, cut five simple petal shapes out of the felt fabric that was cut away in Step 7.

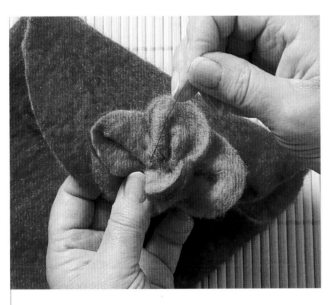

10 Following the manufacturer's instructions, attach one side of the magnetic clasp to the inside of the front flap and the other side to the front of the bag, ensuring that the two sides are exactly opposite one another. Sew the flower to the front flap, covering the back of the clasp.

11 Using the beading needle and thread, sew some of both types of bead onto the center of the flower. Don't try to make a perfect circle, an uneven shape will look more natural. Sew some seed beads onto the edges of one or two of the petals to decorate them further.

Striped satchel

A stylish satchel to take you from the working week to weekends away. This bag looks so good that no one will ever guess how easy it is to knit.

YOU WILL NEED

- One 5 oz (140 g) hank of Peace Fleece Russian American in each of purple (A), mauve (B), and yellow (C)
- US 13 (9 mm) 32 in (80 cm) circular needle
- Pair of US 10 (6 mm) double-pointed needles
- Tape measure
- Knitter's sewing needle

TECHNIQUES

- Knitting for felting, page 110.
- I-cords, page 114.
- Felting knitting in the washing machine, page 111.
- Drying a felted item, page 111.

Finished size approximately 14 x 12 in (35 x 30 cm); strap measures 20 in (50 cm).

Abbreviations page 125.

To make
Satchel

Note Work with two strands of yarn together throughout.

Using US 13 (9 mm) needle and A, loosely cast on 38 sts.
Working back and forth, knit 7 rows garter stitch.
Pick up sides
Pick up 6 sts along first row-edge,

38 sts along opposite long edge, and 6 sts along second row-edge. (88 sts)
Place marker at round end.
Working in the round, knit 65 rounds in stripe patt as folls:
8 rounds A.
8 rounds B.
3 rounds A.
3 rounds C.
3 rounds A.
8 rounds B.
8 rounds A.
5 rounds C.
5 rounds A.
3 rounds B.
3 rounds A.
8 rounds C.
Shape flap
Next round: Using C, k38 then loosely bind off 50 sts. (38 sts)
Working back and forth on these 38 sts, work 45 rows st st in stripe patt as folls:
5 rows A.
5 rows B.
8 rows A.
3 rows C.
8 rows A.
8 rows B.
8 rows C.
Bind off loosely.

Strap
Using US 13 (9 mm) needle and C, loosely cast on 10 sts.
Work in st st in stripe patt as folls:
15 rows C.
15 rows B.
Rep until strap measures 59 in (150 cm) long.
Bind off loosely.

Trimming
Measure around the flap and the open top of the bag.
Using US 10 (6 mm) double-pointed needles and B, cast on 4 sts.
Work an I-cord the measured length, plus 3 in (8 cm).
Bind off.

Making up
Weave in any loose ends. Using the knitter's needle and one strand of B, and starting at the bottom right-hand corner of the flap, neatly sew the I-cord around the edge of the flap and open top of the bag. When you reach the starting point, coil the remaining 3 in (8 cm) of I-cord up and sew it to the corner of the flap (see photograph below).

Felting
Roll up the strap and pin it together to prevent tangling. Following the instructions for Felting Knitting in the Washing Machine, machine-wash the knitting to felt it. When the felting process is complete, follow the instructions for Drying a Felted Item, putting an object of a suitable size (a large book or telephone directory wrapped in a plastic bag works well for this project) inside the bag to help shape it while it dries.

Finishing
When the bag is dry, sew one end of the strap to the inside tops of the two short open sides of the bag, using the sewing needle and thread.

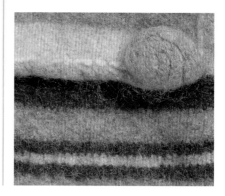

Summer bag

The colors used give this bag a lovely fresh look, though you can make it in other color combinations to create different effects. Try black and white for a sophisticated look, or bright pink and scarlet for a burst of glorious color.

YOU WILL NEED

- One 3½ oz (100 g) ball of Cascade 220 in each of blue (A) and white (B)
- Pair of US 10 (6 mm) double-pointed needles
- US 10 (6 mm) 32 in (80 cm) circular needle
- Knitter's sewing needle
- Magnetic bag clasp

TECHNIQUES

- Knitting for felting, page 110.
- I-cords, page 114.
- Felting knitting in the washing machine, page 111.
- Drying a felted item, page 111.

Finished size approximately 8 x 6¼ in (20 x 16 cm), excluding handles.

Abbreviations page 125.

To make
Bag

Using US 10 (6 mm) double-pointed needles and A, cast on 3 sts.
Work 6 rows of I-cord.
Row 7: K1, inc, k1. (4 sts)
Working on these 4 sts, work 19 in (48 cm) of I-cord. Mark the last row with a safety pin.
Work 100 more rows of I-cord. Mark the last row with a safety pin.
Work a further 16 in (40 cm) of I-cord.
Next row: K1, k2tog, k1. (3 sts)
Working on these 3 sts, work a further 6 rows of I-cord.
Bind off.

Pick up sides
Using US 10 (6 mm) circular needle and B, pick up 84 sts from the I-cord between the two safety pins.
Place marker at round end.
Round 1: K14B, k1A, k69B.
Round 2: K13B, k3A, k68B.
Round 3: K12B, k5A, k67B.
Round 4: K11B, k7A, k66B.
Round 5: K10B, k9A, k65B.
Break A.
Knit 25 rounds in B.
Change to A and knit 24 rounds.
Shape base
Round 55: Bind off 42 sts, k27, bind off 14 sts.
Break yarn.
Rejoin yarn to rem 28 sts and work 14 rows garter stitch.
Bind off loosely.

Flowers
(make two)

Working back and forth on the circular needles and using B, make the flowers following the pattern for Flower 1 on page 85.

Making up

Weave in any loose ends. Using the knitter's needle and A, sew the base to the sides around the three open edges.
Sew the ends of the I-cord to the top of the bag, where the safety pins were, to make two decorative loops.

Felting

Put the flowers in a separate laundry bag. Following instructions for Felting Knitting in the Washing Machine, machine-wash the knitting to felt it. When the felting process is complete, follow the instructions for Drying a Felted Item, putting an object of a suitable size (a thick book wrapped in plastic works well for this project) into the bag to help shape it while it dries.

Finishing

When the bag is dry, attach one side of the clasp to the inside center of each long side of the bag, following the manufacturer's instructions and ensuring that the two sides of the clasp are exactly opposite one another.
Sew a flower trimming over the back of each side of the clasp to hide it.

Silky shoe bag

Keep precious party shoes safe in this beautiful silk and merino bag. Make it to any size you wish and decorate it to match the shoes lucky enough to live in it.

YOU WILL NEED

- Plastic resist, template on page 123
- Towel and bamboo mat
- Black merino fibers
- Sprinkling bottle of warm soapy water
- Piece of fine mesh fabric
- Piece of metallic silk organza twice the size of the resist, plus ¾ in (2 cm) all around
- Fabric marker
- Sewing machine and thread
- Scissors
- Silk fibers
- Embroidery needle and thread

TECHNIQUES

- Felting over a resist, page 116.
- Felting on fabric, page 119.
- Drying a felted item, page 111.

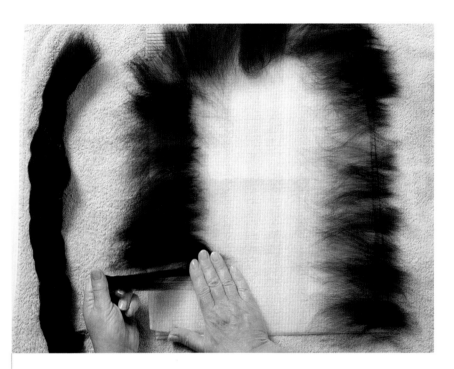

1 Enlarge the template until it is 30 per cent larger than you want the finished shoe bag to be and cut out a plastic resist. Lay the towel on the work surface and place the bamboo mat on top of it. Lay the resist on top of the mat. Place a fringe of fibers around the long sides and curved bottom of the resist, then cover the rest of it with two layers of fibers placed at right-angles to one another.

2 Soak the fibers with warm soapy water from the bottle.

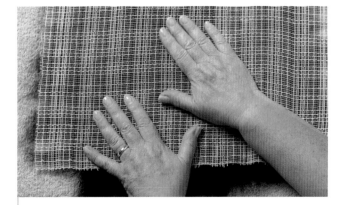

3 Lay the mesh fabric over the wet fibers and gently rub over the net to create a lather. Rub just enough to hold the fibers together; they do not need to be fully felted at this stage.

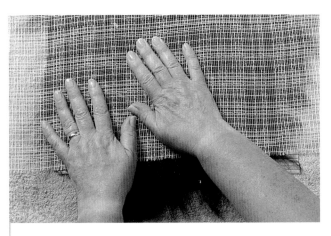

4 Carefully lift the net off the fibers and turn the resist over. Gently flip the fringe of fibers over onto the plastic and smooth them down. Do not flip over any fibers on the short straight (top) edge of the resist.

5 Repeat Steps 1–4 to cover the other side of the resist with fibers in the same way.

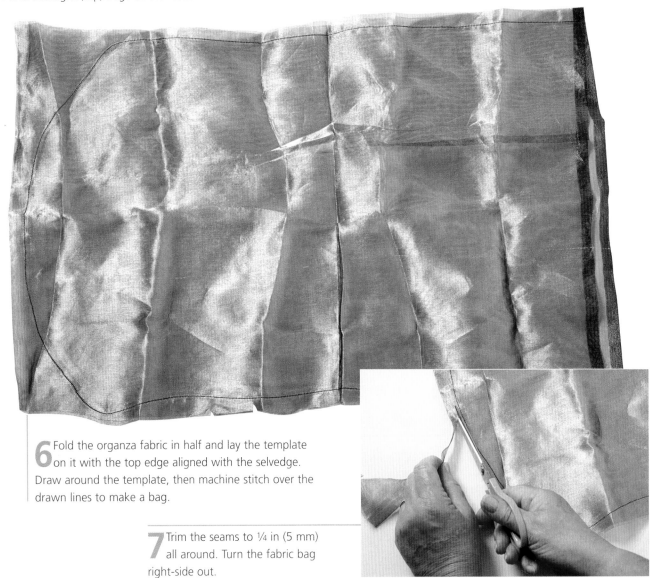

6 Fold the organza fabric in half and lay the template on it with the top edge aligned with the selvedge. Draw around the template, then machine stitch over the drawn lines to make a bag.

7 Trim the seams to ¼ in (5 mm) all around. Turn the fabric bag right-side out.

8 Roll the long sides of the felted shape towards the center to form a tube.

9 Bottom end first, slip the felt tube into the fabric bag. You need to do this in one quick, clean movement to prevent the wet felt snagging on the fabric. Once the felt is right inside the fabric bag, adjust it so that the two shapes fit together.

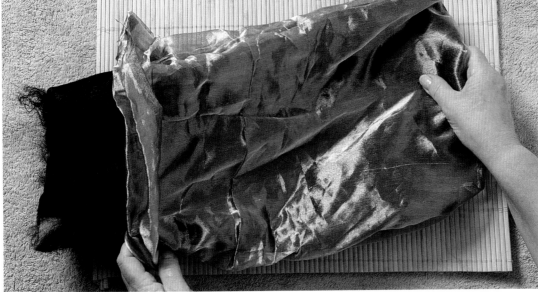

10 Sprinkle the fabric with warm soapy water from the bottle until it is soaked.

11 Rub the fabric to meld the felt inner to it: you will feel the felt start to grip onto the fabric. Work quite gently as you do not want the felt shape to move inside the fabric bag.

12 Lay silk fibers over the lower part of the bag.

13 Decorate the bag further with some wisps of black merino.

Lay some wisps of merino fibers over the edges of the silk fibers to help meld the silk to the fabric.

14 Lay the mesh fabric over the wet fibers and gently rub over it to create a lather. Carefully lift off the mesh and set it aside.

15 Roll up the bag in the bamboo mat and roll the mat back and forth 40 times. Roll up the mat the other way and roll it back and forth a further 40 times to complete the felting process.

Roll the mat up as tightly as you can so that the fabric does not move around inside the roll too much.

16 Slide the plastic resist out of the open end of the bag. Rinse the bag in cold water then in warm water. Leave it flat to dry.

All the silk and merino fibers, on both the inside and outside of the bag, should be felted firmly onto the fabric by this stage. If any of the fibers are loose, roll the bag up in the mat and repeat Step 15 before removing the resist.

17 Thread the embroidery needle with embroidery thread and double it. Work a line of gathering stitches around the bag, about 1½ in (4 cm) down from the top edge. Knot the ends of the thread together to make a drawstring for the bag.

Weekend bag

This wonderful carpet bag lets you travel in style on a weekend away, holding all your beauty essentials and looking good at the same time.

YOU WILL NEED

- Six 1¾ oz (50 g) balls of Twilley Freedom in black (A) and one ball in each of green (B), fuchsia pink (C), and pale pink (D)
- Small amount of Wendy Roxy in pink/green (E)
- US 11 (8 mm) 32 in (80 cm) circular needle
- Knitter's needle
- Black bamboo handles

TECHNIQUES

- Knitting for felting, page 110.
- Felting knitting in the washing machine, page 111.
- Drying a felted item, page 111.

Finished size approximately 12 x 10 in (30 x 25 cm).

Abbreviations page 125.

To make
Bag

Using A, cast on 32 sts.
Working back and forth, knit 76 rows in stripe patt as folls:
14 rows A.
(1 row B, 1 row A) rep 12 times.
2 rows A.
4 rows B.
6 rows A.
8 rows B.
2 rows A.
2 rows B.
14 rows A.

Pick up sides

Using A, pick up 40 sts along first row-edge, 32 sts along opposite edge, and 40 sts along second row-edge. (144 sts)
Place marker at round end.
Knit 8 rounds.
Knit a further 58 rounds, placing 56-row charted flower as you wish.

Make channels

Next round: Bind off 32 sts, k39, bind off 32 sts, k to end.
Working on second group of 40 sts and working back and forth, *knit 8 rows garter stitch.
Bind off.*

Rejoin yarn to rem 40 sts.
Rep from * to *.

Making up

Weave in any loose ends. Fold the two garter stitch strips in and, using the knitter's needle and A, sew the bound off edges to the last row of st st to make channels. Using the knitter's needle and B, work blanket stitch along the two short open edges of the bag.

Felting

Following the instructions for Felting Knitting in the Washing Machine, machine-wash the knitting to felt it. When the felting is complete, follow the instructions for Drying a Felted Item.

Finishing

When the bag is dry, slide the bamboo handles through the channels, following the manufacturer's instructions.

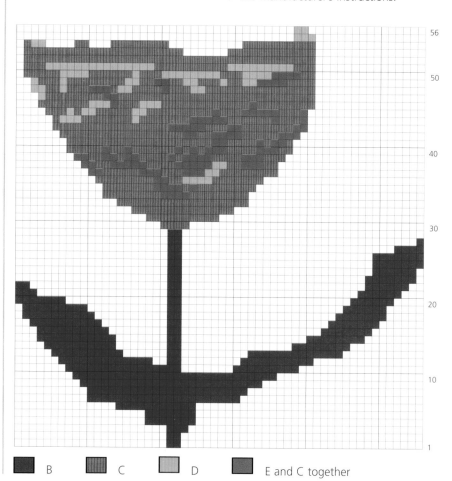

| | B | | C | | D | | E and C together |

Pretty pastel bag

A simple but chic bag that will look as good with a party dress as it will with casual day wear. You'll want to make one to match all your favorite outfits.

YOU WILL NEED

- One 3½ oz (100 g) hank of Debbie Bliss Maya in brown (A)
- One 1¾ oz (50 g) ball of Tahki Poppy in white/browns (B)
- US 15 (10 mm) 32 in (80 cm) circular needle
- Pair of US 8 (5 mm) double-pointed needles
- Knitter's sewing needle
- Magnetic bag fastening
- Two decorative buttons
- Sewing needle and thread

TECHNIQUES

- Knitting for felting, page 110.
- I-cords, page 114.
- Felting knitting in the washing machine, page 111.
- Drying a felted item, page 111.

Finished size approximately 10 x 6¾ in (25 x 17 cm), excluding handles.

Abbreviations page 125.

To make
Bag

Using US 15 (10 mm) needle and A, loosely cast on 34 sts.
Working back and forth, knit 34 rows garter stitch.
Pick up sides
Pick up 16 sts along first row-edge, 34 sts along opposite long edge and 16 sts along second row-edge. (100 sts)
Place marker at round end.
Working in the round, knit 44 rounds.
Join in B and knit 30 rounds with both yarns.
Break B.
Knit 26 rounds in A only.
Bind off loosely.

Handle

Using US 8 (5 mm) double-pointed needles and A, cast on 5 sts.
Work a 30 in (76 cm) I-cord.
Bind off.

Making up

Weave in any loose ends. On the top edge of the bag, fold the center point of one short side in so that the corners meet. Push one end of the I-cord through the four layers of knitted fabric, approximately 4 stitches in from the edge and 6 rows down from the top. Repeat on the other side, threading the other end of the I-cord through. Using the knitter's needle and A, neatly sew the ends of the I-cord together.

Felting

Following the instructions for Felting Knitting in the Washing Machine, machine-wash the bag to felt it. When the felting process is complete, shape the bag with your hands, squaring up the base and folding in the short sides. Pull the I-cord handle a short way through the bag fabric to ensure that the two do not felt together.
Follow the instructions for Drying a Felted Item, putting an object of a suitable size (a milk carton filled with water works well for this project) into the bag to help shape it while it dries.

Finishing

When the bag is dry, attach one side of the clasp to the inside center of each long side of the bag, following the manufacturer's instructions.
Sew a button over the back of each side of the clasp to hide it.

Variation

This version of the Pretty Pastel Bag was made in exactly the same way, but using a different mix of yarns. Those used here are:
- One 1¾ oz (50 g) ball of Texere DK Pure Wool in violet (A)
- One 1¾ oz (50 g) ball of Tahki Poppy in pink (B)

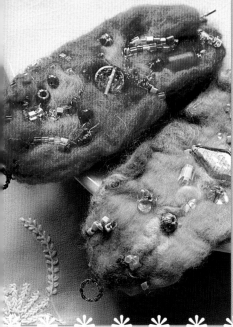

* 2 *
# Jewelry

Pink bobble necklace

Vibrant, colorful felt bobbles are combined with metallic wire and glass beads to create a sophisticated piece of jewelry with designer style.

YOU WILL NEED

- Two large and one smaller bobble made from variegated pink yarn
- 1/16 in (0.2 mm) and 1/8 in (0.5 mm) brass metal wire
- Wire cutters
- US D (3.25 mm) crochet hook
- Round-nosed beading pliers
- Selection of flat glass beads
- Four metal beads
- Two 24 in (60 cm) pieces of 1/2-in (1-cm) wide double-sided satin ribbon

TECHNIQUES

- Felted yarn bobbles, page 114.
- Drying a felted item, page 111.

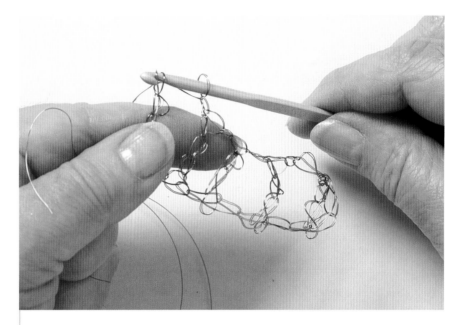

1 Using the crochet hook and fine wire, crochet a simple wire mesh. Make a foundation of 8 chains and work rows of doubles until the mesh is large enough to wrap around a large bobble. Don't worry if the crochet stitches are not very even; an irregular mesh works well.

2 Wrap the mesh around a bobble, pressing it against the yarn so that it's a snug fit. Thread the ends of the wire through stitches to hold the mesh firmly in place. Repeat Steps 1–2 to cover the remaining two bobbles with mesh.

3 Cut a length of thick wire the circumference of your neck. Push one end of the wire right through the yarn bobble a short distance.

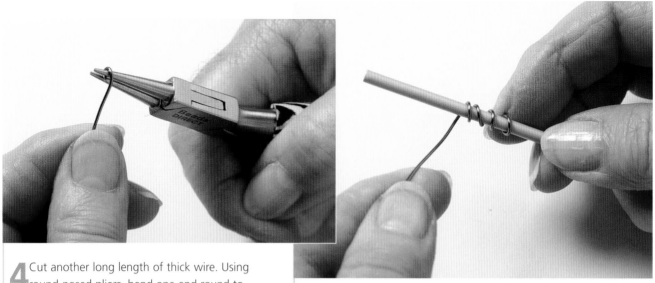

4 Cut another long length of thick wire. Using round-nosed pliers, bend one end round to form a tiny loop.

5 Slip the loop onto the handle of the crochet hook. Wind the wire firmly around the hook about four times to make a little coil.

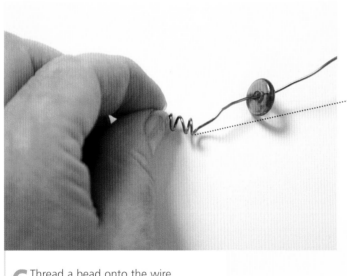

You can make a fairly open coil, as shown here, or a tighter one, more like a spring, if you prefer that effect.

6 Thread a bead onto the wire and slide it down to the top of the coil.

This is the piece of wire that was pushed through the bobble in Step 3.

This is the coiled wire with the bead threaded onto it.

7 Slip the coil and bead over the end of the wire protruding from the yarn bobble.

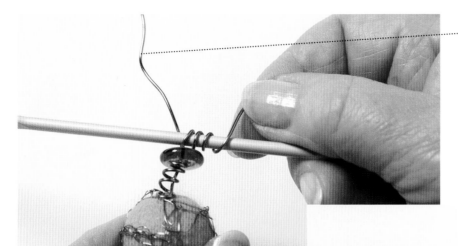

This is the piece of wire that was pushed through the bobble in Step 3. The piece being coiled around the crochet hook is the end of the length in which you made the first coil.

8 Wind the free end of the wire with the bead around the crochet hook to make another coil.

9 Thread on another bead and slip coil and bead over the end of the bobble wire, pulling it through the bobble a little further. Repeat Steps 8–9 until about 2½ in (6.5 cm) of the bobble wire is covered with coils and beads.

10 Pull the bobble wire through until about 4 in (10 cm) of it has passed through the bobble. Cut the coil wire to the same length. Using the fine wire, bind firmly around the two thick wires just above the last bead.

You can use any decorative metal bead, or special findings sold for finishing jewelry.

11 Slide a metal bead onto each end of the thick wire.

12 Using the pliers, bend one end of the wire into a tiny circle. Thread the other end through the loop, then bend it round to join the ends together and form a loop.

13 Fold one length of ribbon in half and slip the folded end through the wire loop. Tuck the free ends through the folded end and pull tight.

When the necklace is fastened by tying the ends of the ribbons in a bow, both sides will show, so the ribbon needs to be double-sided.

The glass beads that lie on the wire between the bobbles are not separated by wire coils.

14 Thread three glass beads onto the end of the wire protruding from the other side of the bobble. Thread on the smaller bobble, three more beads, then the second larger bobble. Repeat Steps 4–13 to complete the other end of the necklace.

Variation

This necklace is made using yarn bobbles threaded onto stringing cord. Thread a long, large-eyed needle with the cord and push the needle through the bobbles. A large metal bead sits between each bobble and the ends of the cord have colored beads and a charm threaded onto them to complete the necklace.

Felted band bracelet

These gorgeous, richly textured bracelets are one of the easiest projects in this book. Decorate your bracelet with beads, pieces recycled from broken vintage jewelry, and pretty charms.

YOU WILL NEED

- Towel, bamboo mat, and bubblewrap
- Merino fibers in two colors
- Sprinkling bottle of warm soapy water
- Piece of fine mesh fabric
- Selection of beads in colors to match fibers
- Beading needle and thread
- Circle and bar fastening

TECHNIQUES

- Felting with fibers, page 116.
- Drying a felted item, page 111.

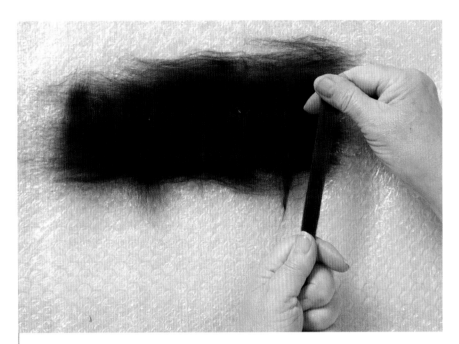

1 Lay the towel then the bamboo mat on the work surface and place the bubblewrap, bubble-side up, on top of the mat. Lay out a band of one color of fibers, laying them in one direction only. Make the band 30 per cent longer than your wrist measurement and whatever width you wish. Then lay a second layer on top of the first, placing the sections at right-angles to the first layer.

2 Lay on a third layer of fibers, of the second color, laying them in the same direction as the first layer.

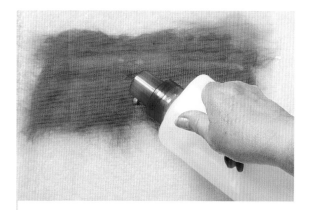

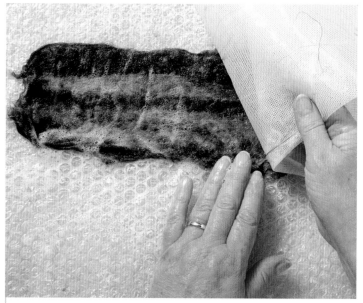

3 Lay the mesh fabric over the fibers and soak them with warm soapy water from the bottle. Very gently, rub the fibers just enough to hold them together.

4 Carefully remove the mesh fabric without disturbing the wet fibers.

The edges of the bracelet will be naturally uneven, but flip over any stray fibers to avoid a shaggy edge.

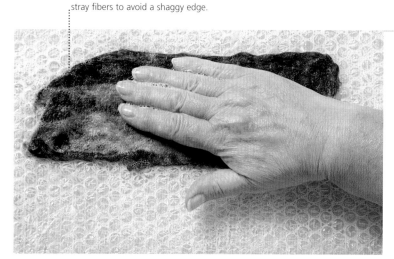

5 Turn the felt over and sprinkle on more soapy water. Flick any loose fibers around the edges over to this (back) side. Replace the mesh and gently rub again to felt the fibers together fully. Leave the felt flat to dry.

6 Arrange the beads on the felt to best effect. If you have a digital camera or cell phone camera, take a picture of the final bead arrangement to refer back to.

7 Using the beading needle and thread, sew the circle part of the fastener to one end of the felt band and the bar part to the other end.

8 Sew the beads onto the felt, securing the thread on the back when you have finished.

Variations

These bracelets look good if all the elements are in shades of the same color. You can try combining colors, but be careful that the bracelet doesn't end up looking too crazy.

Beautiful blue bracelet

Soft blue felted yarn is combined with brilliantly colored glass cane beads to create a striking contemporary bracelet.

YOU WILL NEED

- 1¾ oz (50 g) of pale blue alpaca yarn
- Bowl of warm soapy water
- Glass cane beads in colors to tone with the yarn
- 7-strand flexible beading wire
- Silver crimps
- Crimping pliers
- Bracelet clasp

TECHNIQUES

- Felted yarn bobbles, page 114.
- Drying a felted item, page 111.

1 The felt rods in this bracelet are made using the same technique as a yarn bobble, they are just a different shape. Wind a length of alpaca yarn around your fingers about 20 times.

2 Twist the wound yarn into a figure-of-eight shape, leaving one end of yarn free.

3 Wind the free end of the yarn tightly around the middle of the bundle to hold it together while you felt it.

4 Dip the bundle of yarn into the soapy water, making sure that it is thoroughly soaked.

5 Roll the wet bundle of yarn between your hands to start the felting process.

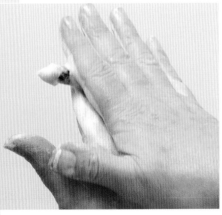

6 As you roll, the yarn will lather up and you will be able to feel the separate strands felting together into a single piece. Make nine felt rods and leave them to dry.

It's the contrast between the irregular, soft alpaca yarn rods and the brightly colored, smooth glass beads that give this bracelet its contemporary impact. The beads used here are of various shades of blue—from pale duck-egg blue to deep blue—with accents of bright green and white. You can, of course, choose different-colored yarn to work with and select beads in a different colorway, but try to keep the same balance of textures and tones. For example, pale pink yarn rods could be interspersed with beads in shades of hot pink, scarlet, and crimson, or lemon-yellow rods with egg-yellow, lime green, and white glass beads. Do experiment with different color combinations: if you don't like the finished arrangement you can always pull the wire out and start again. as threading the bracelet up is not a long or complicated task.

..........Don't worry about making all the yarn rods identical; slight variations in length and thickness are part of the effect.

7 Cut a length of beading wire measuring twice the circumference of your wrist, plus 2 in (5 cm). Start threading up the bracelet, pushing the end of the wire through a felt rod just to one side of the halfway point. Then thread on another bead, then another rod, and so on.

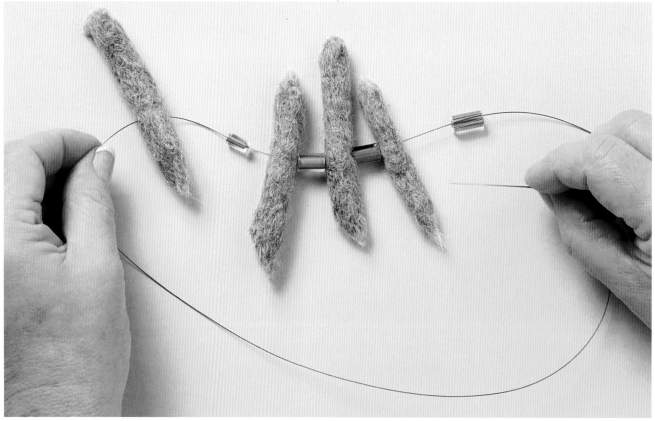

8 Once you have threaded on the last bead, slip a crimp onto the wire, slide it up to sit next to the bead, and squash it with the pliers.

9 Thread one end of the clasp onto the wire, then a bead. Take the wire back through the rods to one side of where it first went through, sliding on a bead between each rod.

10 To fasten on the other end of the clasp, slide a crimp bead onto each end of the wire. Thread the clasp onto one end of the wire, then thread that end through the crimp on the other end of wire. Thread the free end of wire through the clasp and through the opposite crimp, as shown. Pull the ends tight to push the clasp up next to the beads and squash the crimps firmly to hold them in place. Cut off the excess wire very close to the crimps.

Bead and bobble bracelet

This is a really simple bracelet to make; once the bobbles are dry it takes just a few minutes to thread them up. You can use any kind of bead between the bobbles, but if the beads are large you'll need fewer of both them, and the bobbles.

YOU WILL NEED

- Black shirring elastic
- Scissors
- Large-eyed needle
- Seven medium and two small bobbles made from blue alpaca yarn
- Thirteen flat beads

TECHNIQUES

- Felted yarn bobbles, page 114.
- Drying a felted item, page 111.

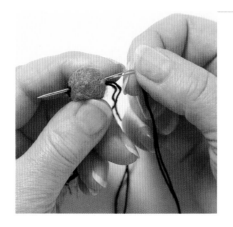

1 Cut a length of elastic three times the circumference of your wrist and thread the needle. Double the elastic and knot it, about 2 in (5 cm) from the cut ends. Push the needle through the middle of a small felt bobble.

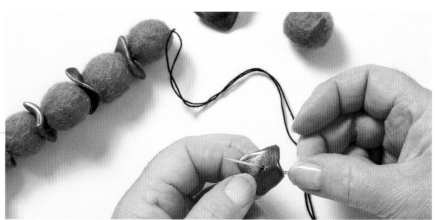

2 Thread on a bead and then a medium bobble. Continue until all the bobbles and nine beads are threaded onto the elastic, finishing with the second small bobble, then a bead.

3 Take the needle through the first bobble again, then through a couple more bobbles and beads. Pull the elastic up taut and check that the bracelet comfortably fits your wrist.

If you wish, you can make one or more of the bobbles from a different-colored yarn to add detail to the bracelet.

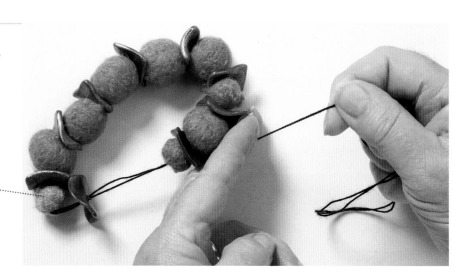

4 Bring the needle and elastic out through a bobble and thread on the remaining four beads.

5 Knot the elastic below the last bead. Take the needle through the knot, then through the four beads and the first couple of bobbles on the bracelet. Cut the end of the elastic between two bobbles.

Tube knit necklace

This organic-looking necklace can be shaped and decorated in a multitude of ways to make a piece that is unique to you. Use beads, pieces from old jewelry, and charms to customize your creation.

INGREDIENTS

- ⅛ in (0.5 mm) and ¹⁄₁₆ in (0.2 mm) pink metal wire
- Wire cutters
- One 1¾ oz (50 g) ball of Colinette Point 5 yarn in pink
- Pair of US 11 (8 mm) double-pointed needles
- Towel and bamboo mat
- Sprinkling bottle of warm soapy water
- Sewing needle
- Selection of beads to tone with yarn

TECHNIQUES

- I-cords, page 114.
- Felting knitting by hand, page 112.
- Drying a felted item, page 111.

Abbreviations page 125.

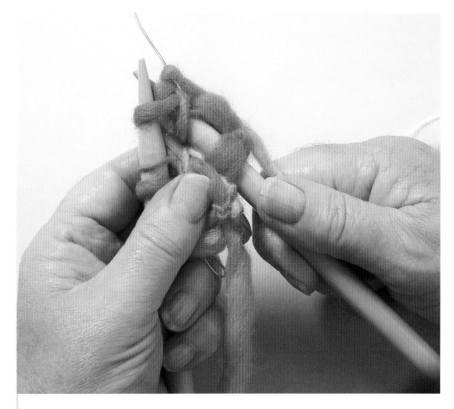

1 Cut a length of thick wire the circumference of your neck plus 10 in (25 cm). Cast on 5 sts and knit the first row of an I-cord. Slide the stitches to the other end of the needle. With your left hand, hold the end of the wire behind the stitches on the needle. As you bring the yarn around from the left to knit the first stitch, ensure that the yarn goes behind the wire. Continue in this way to make an I-cord with the length of wire running down the middle of it. When you have worked a few rows, bend 2 in (5 cm) of the end of the wire over the cast-on edge of the I-cord to prevent it slipping out of the knitting. Work the I-cord until just 2 in (5 cm) of wire protrudes at the other end, then bind off. Fold one free end of the wire in half and bend it to make a loop, then wrap the base of the loop with yarn. Curl the other free end up and wrap it with yarn to make a bobble. Slipping the loop over the bobble fastens the necklace (see main photograph).

2 Lay out the towel and place the bamboo mat on top of it. Lay one end of the I-cord across the mat and sprinkle it with warm soapy water. Roll the cord up in the mat and roll the mat back and forth until the section of cord has felted.

3 Unroll the mat, slide the cord across so an un-felted section is lying on the mat and repeat Step 2. Continue in this way until the whole I-cord is felted.

4 Fold the wet I-cord in half and roll it between your hands to smooth it and form it into a neat tube. Rinse it in cool water, then shape it as you wish and leave the necklace to dry.

5 Thread the needle with fine wire. Decide where you want to put the first bead, then make a couple of stitches through the knitting to anchor the end of the wire.

6 Thread on a bead, then make another stitch through the knitting to hold it in place. Continue adding beads until you are happy with the result.

Variation

This version shows how different the necklace can look in an alternative colorway. Knitted in a wonderful apple-green, blue, and mauve variegated yarn, it is decorated with beads in toning colors.

3
Scarves

Soft chiffon stole

Delicate silk chiffon fabric is combined with pure merino fibers and textured yarn to create this gorgeous stole that will drape softly around your shoulders. Make a wide, long version to wear over a summer evening dress, or choose a narrower style that will coordinate beautifully with pretty day wear.

YOU WILL NEED

- Towel and bubblewrap
- Silk chiffon stole (or cut a piece of fabric to the size you require and machine a narrow double hem around all sides to make your own stole)
- White merino fibers
- Small amounts of fancy yarns in colors of your choice
- Scissors
- Piece of fine mesh fabric
- Sprinkling bottle of warm soapy water
- Bar of soap

TECHNIQUES

- Felting on fabric, page 119.
- Drying a felted item, page 111.

1 Lay out the towel and lay the bubblewrap, bubble-side up, on top of it. Lay one end of the stole on the bubblewrap. Place a layer of fibers in one direction across the fabric, covering about 12 in (30 cm) from the hem up.

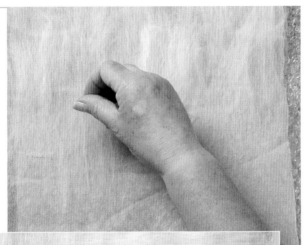

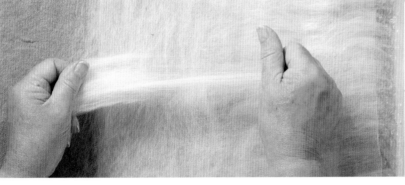

2 Place a second layer of fibers at right-angles to the first layer.

3 Cut 20 in (50 cm) lengths of yarn, fold them in half and lay them on the fibers. The ends of each piece should hang over the end of the stole, as shown.

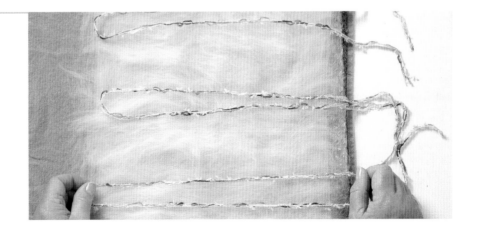

4 Snip off very short pieces of yarn and scatter them over the fibers.

5 Carefully lay the mesh fabric over the fibers and yarn. Pat and smooth the fibers with your hands to push the yarn into them a little before you start felting.

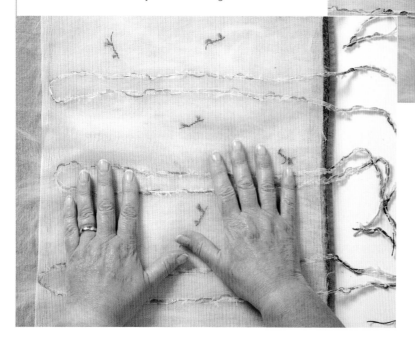

6 Sprinkle on the soapy water, making sure the fibers and yarn are soaked.

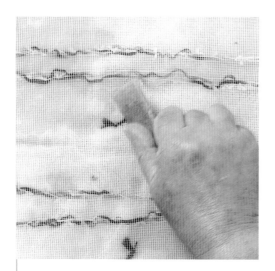

7 Gently rub over the mesh with the bar of soap. Be careful not to disturb the arrangement of fibers and yarn.

8 Start rubbing through the mesh. Work gently at first and then, as the felting process starts, more firmly. Continue until the fibers and yarn are completely felted onto the fabric. Remove the mesh and leave to dry.

Variation

This smaller scarf is made of hand-dyed chiffon, giving it
a lovely soft look. Silvery yarn and tiny flecks of color
enhance the light, ethereal effect.

Knitted mesh scarf

This scarf uses a clever stitch to make a square mesh rather than the slanting hole created by the usual eyelet stitch. It's an easy project to make as the wonderful yarn does all color work for you.

YOU WILL NEED

- One 1¾ oz (50 g) hank of Felt Studio yarn in Siri
- Pair of US 11 (8 mm) needles
- Knitter's sewing needle

TECHNIQUES

- Knitting for felting, page 110.
- Felting knitting by hand, page 112.

Finished size approximately 45 x 8 in (115 x 20 cm)

Abbreviations MS = mesh stitch. Yo, insert needle into next stitch as if to purl it, but catch the stitch beyond and pull this through the first stitch. Knit the pulled-through stitch and slip both stitches off the needle.

See also page 125.

To make
Scarf
Loosely cast on 30 sts.
Knit 7 rows garter stitch.
Next row: K7, MS 16 sts, k7.
Next row: Knit.
Rep these last 2 rows 77 more times.
Knit 7 rows garter stitch.
Bind off loosely.

Making up
Weave in any loose ends.

Felting
Following the instructions for Felting Knitting by Hand, felt the scarf. When the felting process is complete, follow the instructions for Drying a Felted Item, laying the scarf flat to dry.

Silk and cashmere scarf

Wonderfully soft and luxurious to the touch, this elegant scarf will look fabulous with a gorgeous dress or stylish top. Though it isn't worked over a resist, the felting principle is the same, so it's not a difficult project to make.

1 Lay out the towel, lay the mat on top of it, and then the bubblewrap, bubble-side up. Spread out the silk fibers, pulling them out to the length and width you want the scarf to be: this one is 78 in (2 m) long by 8 in (20 cm) wide. Don't try to make a straight-edged, regular shape; the uneven edges are part of the look of this project.

2 Place a layer of cashmere fibers over the silk, allowing them to overlap the silk fibers at the edges.

3 Carefully lay the mesh fabric over the fibers. Sprinkle on the soapy water, making sure the fibers are thoroughly soaked.

4 Gently rub over the mesh with the bar of soap. Be careful not to disturb the arrangement of silk and wool fibers. Rub the fibers through the mesh to felt them together. Rub small sections at a time, rubbing each one for about 5 minutes. Once the felting process is complete, rinse the scarf in cool water and leave it flat to dry.

5 Thread the needle with a long length of linen thread and make a knot about 6 in (15 cm) from the end. Working about 2 in (5 cm) in from one long edge, make a 24-in (60-cm) long line of large running stitches up the scarf. Stitch round in a curve to about 2 in (5 cm) from the opposite edge, then stitch down to the end again.

6 Gently pull up the thread to ruche the end of the scarf. When you are happy with the ruching, knot the end of the thread to hold it in place. Thread three glass beads onto each of the two ends of thread, knotting the thread below them to hold them in place. Repeat Steps 5–6 on the other end of the scarf.

Variation

Made in exactly the same way, but on a smaller scale, this scarf buttons around your neck to keep you beautifully snug.

1 To make a buttonhole, use sharp scissors to cut a slit in the scarf. Using the sewing needle and linen thread, work blanket stitch around the edge of the slit to stop it stretching.

2 Sew on a button to fasten the scarf. Add decorative detail by bringing the needle up through the fabric and button and threading on two beads before going down through the opposite hole in the button.

Cravat scarf

This sophisticated scarf fits snugly around your neck to keep you warm as well as looking stylish through the winter months. Here, it's worked in a muted color palette, but experiment with your favorite colors to create your own unique version.

YOU WILL NEED

- One 1¾ oz (50 g) ball of Noro Kureyon in red/pink (A)
- One 1¾ oz (50 g) ball of Twilley Freedom in black (B)
- Pair of US 10½ (7 mm) needles
- US 10½ (7mm) 16 in (40 cm) circular needle
- Knitter's sewing needle
- Sew-on magnetic clasp
- Decorative button
- Sewing needle and thread

TECHNIQUES

- Knitting for felting, page 110.
- Felting knitting in the washing machine, page 111.
- Drying a felted item, page 111.

Finished size approximately 27 x 9½ in (68 x 24 cm) at widest part.

Abbreviations page 125.

To make
Scarf

Using US 10½ (7 mm) straight needles and A, loosely cast on 37 sts.
Knit 36 rows garter stitch.
Change to B.
Next row: K22, turn, p4, turn, k5, turn, p7, turn, knit to end.
Next row: P16, turn, k9, turn, p10, turn, k11, turn, purl to end.
Change to A.
Knit 16 rows garter stitch across all stitches.
Change to B.
Next row: K10, turn, p3, turn, k4, turn, p5, turn, knit to end.
Next row: P26, turn, k8, turn, p8, turn, k7, turn, purl to end.
Change to A.
Knit 16 rows garter stitch across all stitches.
Change to B.
Knit 2 rows.
Change to A.
Next row: [K5, k2tog] rep to last 2 sts, k2. (32 sts)
Next row: Knit.
Next row: [K1, k2tog] rep to last 2 sts, k2. (22 sts)
Next row: K1, [k2tog] to last st, k1. (12 sts)
Next row: K3, p3, k3, p3.
Rep last 2 rows until ribbed section is long enough to fit around your neck, plus 40 per cent.
Bind off.

Pick up edging

Using US 10½ (7 mm) circular needle and B, pick up an odd number of sts in total (approximately one st for every row) around ribbed section of scarf, starting and finishing at the last stripe in B.
Row 1: Knit.
Row 2: [K1, M1] to last st, k1.
Knit 8 rows.
Bind off loosely.

Making up

Weave in any loose ends.

Felting

Following the instructions for Felting Knitting in the Washing Machine, machine-wash the scarf to felt it. When the felting process is complete, follow the instructions for Drying a Felted Item, laying the scarf flat to dry.

Finishing

Sew one side of the magnetic clasp onto the inside of the short end of the scarf and the other side to the front, so that the scarf fastens comfortably around your neck. Sew the decorative button on the front of the short end of the scarf, over the back of the clasp.

Silk and merino shrug

*Bring out your inner artist when creating this beautiful shrug. As
you lay out the wisps of fiber, think of them as brushstrokes of color
and "paint" an abstract picture.*

YOU WILL NEED

- Towel
- Piece of fine silk voile fabric
  measuring the span of your
  arms from wrist to wrist, by the
  circumference of your upper
  arm plus 2½ in (6 cm).
  Machine sew a narrow double
  hem around all edges.
- Merino fibers in three toning
  colors
- Piece of fine mesh fabric
- Sprinkling bottle of warm
  soapy water
- Dressmakers' pins
- Sewing needle and thread
- Six different-shaped pearl
  buttons

TECHNIQUES

- Felting on fabric, page 119.
- Drying a felted item, page 111.

1 Working on a smooth surface, lay out a small section of fibers. Pull out tiny
sections in different colors and lay them side by side to "paint" your design.
The slightest breeze will blow the fibers away, so don't breathe too hard!

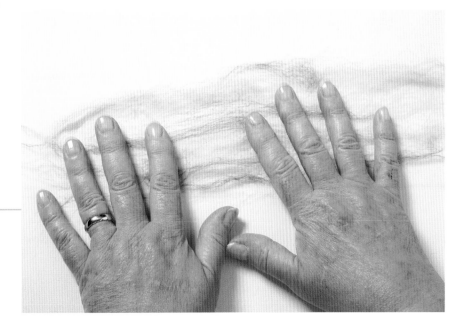

2 When you are happy with the look
of a section, carefully lay your hands
flat on it and very gently move them
around just a little to begin to meld
the fibers together.

3 When the fibers are sufficiently melded, you will be able to carefully pick the section up.

4 On another work surface, lay out the towel and lay the fabric on top of it. As you make the sections of fiber, arrange them on the fabric, gently patting them down with your hands.

5 Very carefully lay the mesh fabric over the fibers without disturbing them. Sprinkle on warm soapy water, making sure the fibers are soaked.

6 Working on a small section at a time, rub the area with the bar of soap and then rub it with your hands for about 10 minutes. Continue in this way until all the fibers are felted onto the fabric.

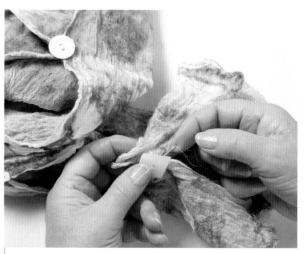

7 When the fabric is dry, mark the points along the long edges with pins where you want to position the buttons. Each arm of the shrug has three buttons; one close to the wrist, one at the elbow and one on the upper arm. Using the needle and thread, sew the long side of the felted fabric together at these points.

8 Sew on a decorative button at each stitched point along the sleeves.

Variation

You can lay sections of fibers at selected points on the fabric, rather than covering the whole piece. Soap and rub each section and as it felts the fabric will pucker up around it to create the pretty effect shown on this scarf.

* **4** *
Accessories

Pretty felt pumps

These ballet pumps are so popular with my customers, who order pairs in colors to match everything from their dressing gowns to the most fabulous party dresses.

To make a template for your pumps

To make a template that lets you make both pumps at the same time, place your left foot on a sheet of paper and draw around it. Measure from heel to toe and mark the center point. From the heel, draw a line out to the right. Draw a parallel line out from the marked center point. About 1 in (3 cm) from the edge of the foot, draw a short line to join the two parallel lines. Draw a second line around the shape, 2 in (5 cm) out from the original line, smoothing out the shape. Cut out the template and lay it on the resist material. Draw around the shape, then flip it over to draw around its mirror image, joining the two shapes at the central and heel lines. On page 120 you will find a sample template to use as a guide when making your own.

YOU WILL NEED

- Towel and bamboo mat
- Plastic resist, see instructions, left and template on page 120.
- Purple, cream, and pink merino fibers
- Sprinkling bottle of warm soapy water
- Piece of fine mesh fabric
- Scissors
- Foot lasts the same size as your feet (see Suppliers)
- Pair of popsocks
- Bar of soap
- Black permanent marker pen
- Dry felting needle

TECHNIQUES

- Felting over a resist, page 116.
- Felting knitting in the washing machine, page 111.
- Drying a felted item, page 111.

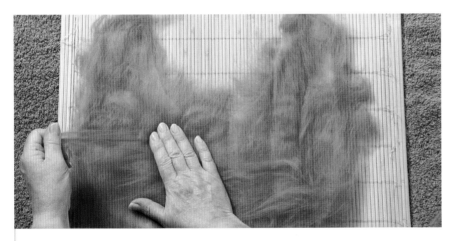

1 Lay the towel then the bamboo mat on the work surface and lay the plastic resist on top of the mat. Cover the resist with small sections of purple fiber, making sure that the fibers overlap the edge of the resist all around and that the plastic is evenly covered.

2 Place a layer of cream fibers over the purple ones, covering all the purple apart from the toes. Lay a second layer of purple fibers over the toes.

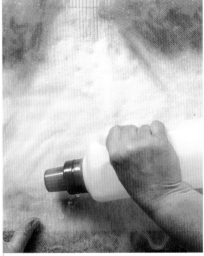

3 Lay the mesh fabric over the fibers, then soak them with warm soapy water from the bottle. Gently rub over the net to create a lather.

4 Lift the net off the fibers and turn the resist over. Gently flip the fringe of fibers over onto the plastic and smooth them down. Repeat Steps 1–4 to cover the other side of the resist with fibers. Soak and lather the fibers as before and flip the fringe of fibers over onto the first side.

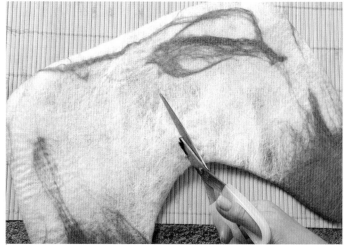

5 Using scissors, cut across one layer of fibers, cutting across the middle of the shape. Turn the shape over and cut the other layer in the same place.

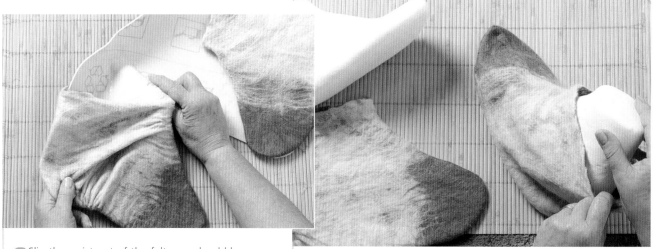

6 Slip the resist out of the felt: you should have two felt boot shapes.

7 Slide a last into each felt boot. The felt boots will be bigger than the lasts at this stage.

8 Rub the bar of soap all over the felt. Then rub firmly with your hands for about 10 minutes on each boot to smooth them onto the last.

9 Slip a popsock over each felt boot and knot the top of the sock on top of the last. Following the instructions for Felting Knitting in the Washing Machine, machine-wash the pumps to felt them. When the felting process is complete, remove the pop socks and leave the pumps on the lasts to dry.

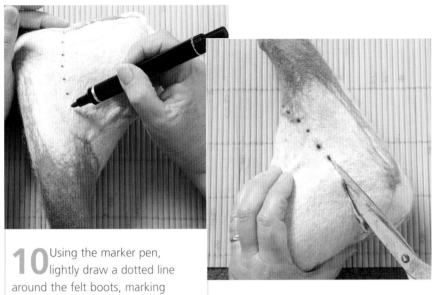

10 Using the marker pen, lightly draw a dotted line around the felt boots, marking where you want the top edge of the pump to be.

11 Cut the felt along the drawn lines with scissors.

12 Lather your hands with warm soapy water and rub along the cut edges to smooth them.

13 Make a small curl of merino fiber to decorate the toes of the pumps.

14 With the lasts still in place, lay the curl in position on the toe of a pump. Stab the curl with the dry felting needle until the fibers are melded into those of the pump (this takes a surprisingly short amount of time).

Variation

If you have polished wooden floors and are worried that your pumps might slip, sew small pieces of the anti-slip material sold for use under rugs onto the soles of the pumps. Sew one piece to the toe and one to the heel and your sliding should stop!

Glitter-edged muff

This is a clever project that uses the way the wool yarn shrinks to create the glitter edging. Also, the muff is reversible; wear it glitter-side out when you want to add a little more sparkle to an outfit.

YOU WILL NEED

- One 1¾ oz (50 g) ball of Twilley Paris Mohair in each of cream (A) and beige (B)
- One 1¾ oz (50 g) ball of Twilley Spirit in brown (C)
- One 1¾ oz (50 g) ball of Twilley Chic in brown (D)
- One 1¾ oz (50 g) ball of Twilley Frizzante in each of brown (E) and cream (F)
- US 10 (6 mm) 32 in (80 cm) circular needle
- Knitter's sewing needle

TECHNIQUES

- Knitting for felting, page 110.
- Felting knitting in the washing machine, page 111.
- Drying a felted item, page 111.

Finished size approximately 12 x 10½ in (30 x 27 cm).

Abbreviations page 125.

To make
Outer
Using A, B, and C, loosely cast on 48 sts. Place marker at round end and join into the round, being careful not to twist sts. Knit until work measures 20 in (50 cm). Bind off loosely.

Inner
Using D, loosely cast on 48 sts. Place marker at round end and join into the round, being careful not to twist sts. Knit until half the ball of yarn has been used.
Break D.
Join in E and F together.
Knit until all the yarn is used.
Join in D.
Knit until all the yarn is used.
Bind off loosely.

Making up
Right-sides facing, slide the outer piece inside the inner piece, aligning the row ends at one end of the muff. Using the knitter's sewing needle and A, sew the aligned ends together. Pull the outer piece out. Wrong sides facing, push the inner piece inside the outer and align the free row ends. Using mattress stitch, sew these ends together.

Felting
Following the instructions for Felting Knitting in the Washing Machine, machine-wash the knitting to felt the muff outer. (The outer part of the muff is made of wool, so it will felt in the machine. The inner part is man-made fibers and will not felt.)
When the felting process is complete, ease out the muff inner so that an equal amount is visible as a trimming at the edge of the felted outer. Fluff up the trimming, then follow the instructions for Drying a Felted Item, leaving the muff flat to dry.

Finishing
Using scraps of toning yarns and following the instructions on page 82, make four woven bobbles. Sew the bobbles to the front of the muff outer to decorate it. If you wish, you can attach a cord or ribbon to the muff to hang it around your neck.

Knitted party pumps

Companions to the Pretty Felt Pumps (see page 74), these knitted felt pumps can be made and decorated in any colors you choose. Decorate the toes as shown here, or knit a flower (see page 85) and sew that on instead.

YOU WILL NEED

- One 3½ oz (100 g) ball of Knitting4fun Chunky in orange
- Small amount of fancy yarn in color of choice for decoration
- US 13 (9 mm) 32 in (80 cm) circular needle
- Knitter's sewing needle
- Plastic foot lasts the same size as your feet (see Suppliers)
- Pair of popsocks
- Weavette (see Suppliers)

TECHNIQUES

- Knitting for felting, page 110.
- I-cords, page 114.
- Felting knitting in the washing machine, page 111.
- Drying a felted item, page 111.

Sizes: Small shoe sizes US 4½–5½ (UK 3–4). **Medium** shoe sizes US 6½–8½ (UK 5–7). **Large** shoe sizes US 8½–10½ (UK 7–9).

Abbreviations WT = wrap and turn. With the yarn at the back, slip the next stitch on the left-hand needle purlwise onto the right-hand needle. Bring the yarn forward. Slip the stitch back onto the left-hand needle and take the yarn back. Turn the work.

See also page 125.

To make
Outer pump (make 2)

**Cast on 48(54:60) sts, placing marker at 24th(27th:30th) st.
Work back and forth.
Row 1: K1, M1, k23(26:29), M1, k1, M1, k17(20:23), WT, k38(44:50), WT, k17(20:23), M1, k2, M1, k1, M1, k2, M1, k21(24:27), M1, k1. (56:62:68 sts)
Row 2: Purl across all sts.
Row 3: K1, M1 k25(28:31), M1, k2, M1, k1, M1, k2, M1 k12(14:16), WT, k34(38:42), WT, k12(14:16), M1, k3, M1, k2, M1, k1, M1, k2, M1, k3, M1, k23(26:29), M1, k1. (68:74:80 sts)
Work 2 rows st st across all sts. Place toe marker at center stitch and marker at round end and join into the round, being careful not to twist stitches.
Knit three rounds.**

Shape toe

Knit 3 rounds.
Next round: K22(25:28), work shaping on next 24 sts only, k4, k2tog, k2, ssk, k4, k2tog, k2, ssk, k4, WT, p2, p2tog, p2, p2tog, p4, p2tog, p2, p2tog, p2, WT, k2tog, k2, ssk, k4, k2tog, k2, ssk, WT, p2tog, p2tog, p4, p2tog, p2tog, WT, ssk, k2tog, ssk, k2tog, knit to end of round.
Knit 2 rounds across all sts.
Bind off.

Inner sole (make 2)

Using 2 strands of yarn, rep instructions from ** to **.
Bind off.

Making up

Weave in any loose ends.
Using the knitter's sewing needle and yarn, sew up the center seams of the outer pumps and inner soles.
With inner sole right-side up, starting at the heel marker and using US 13 (9 mm) circular needle, pick up sts from around the very edge of each sole; pick up 1 st from each garter stitch ridge. Join in a second strand of yarn and bind off.
Using the knitter's sewing needle and yarn, sew the soles to the outer pumps along the center seams.

Felting

Place a foot last in each pump. Slip last and pump inside a popsock and knot the top of the sock on top of the last. Following the instructions for Felting Knitting in the Washing Machine, machine-wash the pumps to felt them. When the felting process is complete, remove the pop socks and follow the instructions for Drying a Felted Item, leaving the pumps on the lasts to dry.

Finishing

A Weavette is a clever little tool that allows you quickly and easily to make bobbles and bows with which to decorate all sorts of felted items.

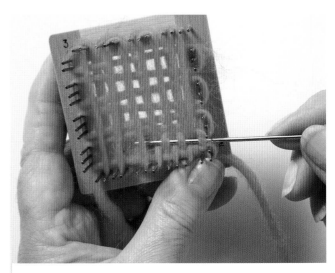

2 Thread the knitter's sewing needle with the end of the yarn. Weave the needle under and over a few strands, pull the yarn through, then weave the needle through again.

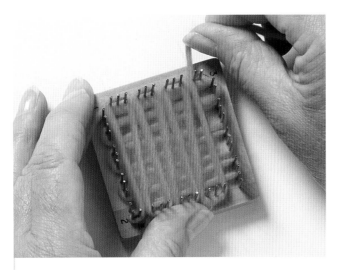

1 Following the instructions that come with the Weavette, wind orange yarn between the nails.

When slipping the square off the nails, be careful to avoid catching any strands of yarn.

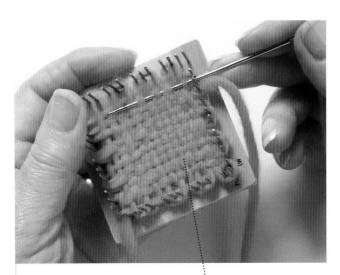

3 Continue until the frame of the Weavette is filled with tightly woven yarn. Leave the threaded tail of yarn to one side.

Use the needle to push the woven rows tightly against one another as you work.

Don't worry about any loops of yarn on the sides of the square, they will disappear when it is made into a bobble.

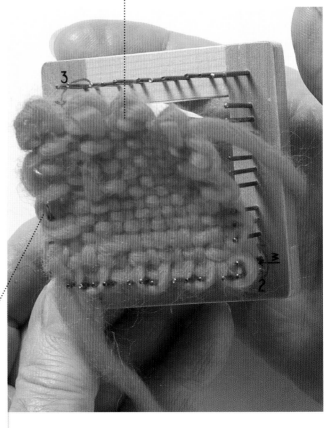

4 Gently ease the woven square off the nails.

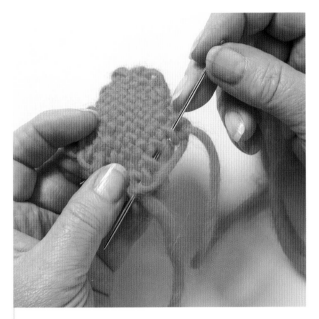

5 Using the threaded tail of yarn, run a line of gathering stitches all around the edges of the woven square.

7 Make another bobble using the fancy yarn. Then make two more woven pieces, one in each yarn, and gather them across the middle to make bows. Stack the four woven pieces on top of one another and stitch them together through the centers using the knitter's needle and orange yarn, and following the photograph.

6 Pull the stitches up tight to turn the square into a three-dimensional bobble.

8 Using the same needle and yarn, sew the stacked decoration to the toe of a pump. Repeat to decorate the toe of the second pump.

Flower tie belt

Wear it with jeans, a summer shift dress, or casual linen trousers and a shirt—it'll look great with all of them, and much more besides. This belt matches the Cool Club Bag (see page 86), but of course you don't need to wear them together.

YOU WILL NEED

- One 1¾ oz (50 g) ball of Texere Alpaca Select in turquoise (A)
- One 1¾ oz (50 g) ball of Kollage Illumination in green (B)
- Pair of US 11 (8 mm) needles
- Pair of US 8 (5 mm) double-pointed needles
- Knitter's sewing needle

TECHNIQUES

- Knitting for felting, page 110.
- I-cords, page 114.
- Felting knitting in the washing machine, page 111.
- Drying a felted item, page 111.

Finished size approximately 1½ in (4 cm) wide.

Abbreviations Twist = turn the point of the left-hand needle right around to the back, under the knitted fabric and back up to the working position, so putting a twist in the knitted fabric.

See also page 125.

To make
Belt
Using US 11 (8 mm) needles and A, cast on 10 sts.
Knit garter stitch until belt is required length, plus 30 per cent.
Bind off.

I-cord trimmings
Using US 8 (5 mm) double-pointed needles and B, cast on 3 sts.
Work four I-cords of different lengths and bind off.

Flowers
Three flower patterns are given here, all producing flowers that are slightly different. Experiment and make three of your favorite flower in yarn B.

Flower 1
- Pair of US 8 (5 mm) needles
Cast on 66 sts.
Knit 4 rows.
Row 5: K6, [twist, k6] rep to end.
Row 6: [P2tog] rep to end. (33 sts)
Row 7: Knit.
Row 8: [P2tog] rep to last st, p1. (17 sts)
Row 9: Knit.
Row 10: [P2tog] rep to last st, p1. (9 sts)
Cut the yarn, leaving a 6 in (15 cm) tail.
Thread the end through the rem 9 sts and pull up tight. Thread the knitter's sewing needle with the tail of yarn and sew the short open ends of the flower together.

Flower 2
- Pair of US 2 (3 mm) needles
Cast on 54 sts.
Knit 4 rows.
Row 5: K6, [twist, k6] rep to end.
Purl 1 row.
Row 7: [K2tog] rep to end. (27 sts)
Row 8: [P2tog] rep to last st, k1. (14 sts)
Row 9: [K2tog] rep to end. (7 sts)
Cut the yarn, leaving a 6 in (15 cm) tail.
Thread the end through the rem 7 sts

and pull up tight. Thread the knitter's sewing needle with the tail of yarn and sew the short open ends of the flower together.

Flower 3
- Pair of US 8 (5 mm) needles
Cast on 42 sts.
Starting with a k row, work 5 rows st st.
Row 6: P6, [twist, p6] rep to end.
Row 7: [P2tog] rep to end. (21 sts)
Row 8: [P2tog] rep to last st, p1. (11 sts)
Cut the yarn, leaving a 6 in (15 cm) tail.
Thread the end through the rem 11 sts and pull up tight. Thread the knitter's sewing needle with the tail of yarn and sew the short open ends of the flower together.

Making up
Using the knitter's sewing needle and yarn B, sew two I-cords and one flower to each end of the belt. Sew the third flower to the free end of an I-cord.

Felting
Fold the belt up and pin it together to stop it tangling. Following the instructions for Felting Knitting in the Washing Machine, machine-wash the belt to felt it.
When the felting process is complete, shape the flowers with your fingers, then follow the instructions for Drying a Felted Item, leaving the belt flat to dry.

Cool club bag

A tiny bag to hold your house key, cash, and lipstick—all you need for a night out. Alternatively, tuck your I-pod into the bag, thread the headphone wires through the buttonhole in the top of the flap, and take your music with you wherever you go.

YOU WILL NEED

- One 1¾ oz (50 g) ball of Texere Alpaca Select in turquoise (A)
- One 1¾ oz (50 g) ball of Kollage Illumination in green (B)
- US 1 (2.25 mm) 16 in (40 cm) circular needle
- Pair of US 8 (5 mm) double-pointed needles
- US D (3.25 mm) crochet hook
- Knitter's sewing needle
- One large bead
- Beading needle and thread

TECHNIQUES

- Knitting for felting, page 110.
- I-cords, page 114.
- Felting knitting in the washing machine, page 111.
- Drying a felted item, page 111.

Finished size approximately 3½ x 5 in (9 x 13 cm), excluding strap.

Abbreviations page 125.

To make
Bag

Using US 1 (2.25 mm) circular needle and A, loosely cast on 22 sts.
Working back and forth, knit 14 rows garter stitch.

Pick up sides

Pick up 7 sts along first row-edge, 22 sts along opposite long edge and 7 sts along second row edge. (58 sts)
Place marker at round end.
Work in the round.
Round 1: K22, [k1, p1] rep twice more, k23, [k1, p1] rep twice more, k1.
Rep this round until work measures 6 in (15 cm).

Shape flap

Next round: K22, bind off rem sts purlwise. (22 sts)
Next row: Knit.
Next row: K7, bind off 8, k to end.
Next row: K7, cast on 8, k to end.
Knit 4 rows garter stitch.
Change to B.
Knit 4 rows garter stitch.
Change to A.
Next row: K3, k2tog, k12, k2tog, k3. (20 sts)
Next row and every alt row: Knit.
Next row: K3, k2tog, k10, k2tog, k3.
Next row: K3, k2tog, k8, k2tog, k3.
Change to B.
Next row: K3, k2tog, k6, k2tog, k3. (14 sts)
Next row: K3, k2tog, k4, k2tog, k3.
Next row: K3, k2tog, k2, k2tog, k3.
Change to A.
Next row: K3, [k2tog] rep once more, k3. (8 sts)

Next row: K2, [k2tog] rep once more, k2.
Next row: K1, [k2tog] rep once more, k1.
Next row: [K2tog] rep once more. (2 sts)
Place these 2 sts on crochet hook and make 10 in (25 cm) chain.

Strap

Using US 8 (5 mm) double-pointed needles and A, cast on 4 sts.
Work an I-cord the desired length of the strap, plus 30 per cent. Bind off.

I-cord trimmings

Using US 8 (5 mm) double-pointed needles and A, cast on 3 sts.
Work three I-cords of different lengths and bind off.

Flower

Using B, make a flower following one of the patterns given in Flower Belt, see page 85.

Making up

Using the knitter's sewing needle and A, sew one end of the I-cord handle to each inside top of the ribbed sides of the bag. Sew the flower to the front of the bag, positioning it centrally and below the point of the flap. Sew one end of the I-cord trimmings to one top edge of the bag.

Felting

Place the bag in a laundry bag. Following the instructions for Felting Knitting in the Washing Machine, machine-wash the bag to felt it. When the felting process is complete, shape the flower with your fingers, then follow the instructions for Drying a Felted Item, leaving the bag flat to dry.

Finishing

Using the beading needle and thread, sew the large bead into the center of the flower. Close the bag by wrapping the cord hanging from the flap around the base of the flower.

5
Hats

Cute winter hat

This fun hat is the perfect solution for keeping little ones warm in even the coldest weather. With a cute design and pretty colors, they'll want to keep it on, too!

YOU WILL NEED

- One 1¾ oz (50 g) ball of Anny Blatt Fleur in pink (A)
- One 1¾ oz (50 g) ball of Rooster in strawberry pink (B)
- US 10 (6 mm) 24 in (60 cm) circular needle
- Knitter's sewing needle

TECHNIQUES

- Knitting for felting, page 110.
- Felting knitting in the washing machine, page 111.
- Drying a felted item, page 111.

Finished size To fit small and large child's heads.

Abbreviations page 125.

To make
Hat

Using A, loosely cast on 72(96) sts.
Place marker at round end. Join into the round, being careful not to twist stitches.
Round 1: Knit. Place markers after 3rd, 32nd, 36th, 47th, 60th (3rd, 44th, 48th, 62nd, 81st) sts.
Shape around face
Round 2: Knit to 36th(48th) st, turn, p8, turn, k8, turn, purl to round end, turn, k8, turn, p8, turn.
Break A and join in B.
Knit two rounds.
Next round: [P4, k4] rep to end.

Rep this round seven more times.
Next round: [P4, k4] rep to end.
Rep this round 10(16) more times.
Next round (RS): Knit.
Rep this round until work measures 6(8) in (15(20) cm) from end of ribbing.
Shape crown
Join in A and work with both yarns.
Next round: [K9(12), k2tog] rep to last 6(12) sts, k6(12). (66:90 sts)
Next round: Knit.
Next round: [K4, k2tog] rep to end. (55:75 sts)
Next round: Knit.
Next round: [K3, k2tog] rep to end. (44:60 sts)
Next round: Knit.
Next round: [K2, k2tog] rep to end. (33:45 sts)
Next round: Knit.
Next round: [K1, k2tog] rep to end. (22:30 sts)
Next round: [K2tog] rep to end. (11:15 sts)
Next round: [K2tog] rep to last st, k1. (6:8 sts)
Cut yarn leaving 6 in (15 cm) tail.
Thread knitter's sewing needle with yarn tail and thread through rem 6(8) sts and pull up tight.
Pick up flaps
Left ear
With RS facing and A, pick up and knit 14(18) sts between 4th(4th) and 60th(81st) sts.
**Working back and forth, work 11(14) rows st st.
Next row: K1, k2tog, k to last 3 sts, ssk, k1. (12:16 sts)
Next row: P1, ssp, p to last 3 sts,

p2tog, p1. (10:14 sts)
Rep last 2 rows till 2 sts rem.
Bind off.**
Right ear
With RS facing and A, pick up and knit 14(18) sts between 32nd(44th) and 47th(62nd) sts.
Rep from ** to **.

Making up
Weave in any loose ends.

Felting
Following the instructions for Felting Knitting in the Washing Machine, machine-wash the hat to felt it.
When the felting process is complete, fluff up the textured yarn then follow the instructions for Drying a Felted Item.

Variation
This version of the Winter Hat is made in muted grays and is ideal for a boy. The yarns used here are:
- One 1¾ oz (50 g) ball of Garnstudio Eskimo in each of pale gray (A) and dark gray (B).

Elegant pink hat

With its dramatic sweeping brim, this hat makes a great style statement whatever the occasion. Customize it with your own added decoration and wear it everywhere.

YOU WILL NEED

- Two 1¾ oz (50 g) balls of Garnstudio Eskimo Tone-in-tone yarn in pinks
- US 15 (10 mm) 32 in (80 cm) circular needle
- Knitter's sewing needle
- Decoration
- Sewing needle and thread

TECHNIQUES

- Knitting for felting, page 110.
- Felting knitting in the washing machine, page 111.
- Drying a felted item, page 111.

Size to fit average adult head.

Abbreviations page 125.

To make
Hat

Loosely cast on 110 sts.
Place marker at round end and join into the round, being careful not to twist stitches.
Knit in rounds until work measures 2 in (5 cm) from cast on edge.
Next round: [K8, k2tog] rep to end of round. (99 sts)
Knit in rounds until work measures 6½ in (16.5 cm) from cast on edge.

Next round: K2tog, [k3, k2tog] rep to last 2 sts, k2. (79 sts)
Next round: K2tog, k24, k2tog, k23, k2tog, k24, k2tog. (75 sts)
Knit in rounds until work measures 12 in (30 cm) from cast on edge.
Next round: [K2tog, k3] rep to end. (60 sts)
Knit 2 rounds.
Next round: [K2tog, k2] rep to end. (45 sts)
Knit 2 rounds.
Rep last 6 rounds once more. (27 sts)
Next round: [K2tog, k1] rep to end. (18 sts)
Knit 2 rounds.
Next round: [K2tog] rep to end. (9 sts)
Cut yarn leaving 6 in (15 cm) tail. Thread knitter's sewing needle with yarn tail, thread through rem 9 sts and pull up tight. Make a couple of stitches on the inside of the hat to secure the knitting.

Making up
Weave in any loose ends.

Felting
Following the instructions for Felting Knitting in the Washing Machine, machine-wash the hat to felt it. When the felting process is complete, follow the instructions for Drying a Felted Item.

Finishing
At the front of the hat, fold up the brim to touch the crown and sew the decoration in place, sewing the brim to the crown at the same time.

Felt beret with flower

A great way to create a unique felt piece is to have fibers dyed to a personal color blend (see Suppliers). These can be colors associated with your hair and skin tones, or just a favorite mix of shades—the choice is yours.

YOU WILL NEED

- Towel and bamboo mat
- Plastic resist, a circle of plastic 30 per cent larger than the desired diameter of the finished beret
- Color-blended merino fibers
- Piece of fine mesh fabric
- Sprinkling bottle of warm soapy water
- Scissors
- Bar of soap
- Sewing needle and thread

TECHNIQUES

- Felting over a resist, page 116.
- Drying a felted item, page 111.

1 Lay out the towel with the bamboo mat on top of it. Place the resist on the mat. Cover the resist with a layer of fibers, starting with a fringe of fibers overlapping the edge of the resist all around.

2 Lay on a second layer of fibers at right-angles to the first layer.

Don't worry about trying to arrange the colored fibers in a particular way, as they'll all blend beautifully when felted.

3 Lay the mesh fabric over the fibers. Sprinkle on warm soapy water to soak the fibers and rub through the mesh to felt them together. Turn the resist over and flip over the fringe of fibers. Repeat Steps 1–3 to cover the other side of the resist with felt.

4 Using scissors, cut out a circle in the middle of one side of the felted resist. The circle should be a little larger than the circumference of your head. Pull the plastic resist out through this opening.

5 Rub the beret all over with the bar of soap. Continue rubbing with your hands to felt the beret even further and shrink it to fit your head.

6 To make the decorative tail, lay a 10-in (25-cm) long section of fiber across one end of the mat. Leave about 2 in (5 cm) protruding over one side of the mat. Sprinkle the fibers on the mat with soapy water so they are thoroughly soaked.

7 Roll up the mat tightly and roll it back and forth under your hands to felt the fibers into a tail.

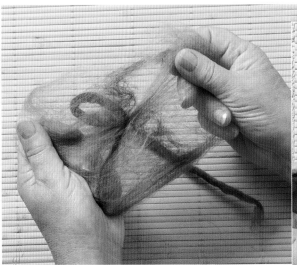

8 Gently tease out the un-felted end of the fibers to make a circle at the base of the tail.

9 Lay this circle on the top of the beret, where you want the tail to sprout from. Sprinkle the circle of loose fibers with soapy water and rub it to felt it onto the beret.

10 Fold the circle of felt cut out in Step 4 into quarters. Snip off the point of the folded triangle with scissors and unfold it again.

11 Thread the free end of the tail through the hole in the felt circle.

12 Pinch the base of the circle around the tail to form a flower. Using the needle and thread, sew the base of the flower to the tail. Once the hat is shaped and dry, you can trim the opening if necessary to fit your head perfectly.

Jaunty bowler

This easy-to-wear bowler-style hat will serve you well through both the summer and winter. Team it with a big coat and toning wool scarf for winter style, or a cotton print dress for a deliciously retro summer look.

YOU WILL NEED

- One 1¾ oz (50 g) ball of Garnstudio Eskimo in green
- Small amount of black pure wool yarn
- US 10 (6 mm) 32 in (80 cm) circular needle
- Knitter's sewing needle

TECHNIQUES

- Knitting for felting, page 110.
- Felted yarn bobbles, page 114.
- Felting knitting in the washing machine, page 111.
- Drying a felted item, page 111.

Size to fit average adult head.

Abbreviations page 125.

To make
Hat

Cast on 106 sts.
Join into the round, being careful not to twist stitches.
Shape brim
Round 1: [K29, k2tog] rep seventeen more times, ignoring round ends. (88 sts)
Place round end marker after last rep.
Knit 23 rounds.
Shape crown
Next round: [K6, k2tog] rep to end. (77 sts)
Next round and foll 4 alt rounds: Knit.

Next round: [K5, k2tog] rep to end. (66 sts)
Next round: [K4, k2tog] rep to end. (55 sts)
Next round: [K3, k2tog] rep to end. (44 sts)
Next round: [K2, k2tog] rep to end. (33 sts)
Next round: [K1, k2tog] rep to end. (22 sts)
Next round: [K2tog] rep to end. (11 sts)
Cut yarn leaving long tail. Thread knitter's sewing needle with tail and take through rem 11 sts and pull up tight. Make a couple of small stitches to secure the knitting, but do not cut off the tail of yarn.

Bobble

Using a mix of green and black yarn and following the instructions for Felted Yarn Bobbles, make a single bobble.

Making up

Weave in any loose ends.

Felting

Following the instructions for Felting Knitting in the Washing Machine, machine-wash the hat to felt it. When the felting process is complete, follow the instructions for Drying a Felted Item.

Finishing

Thread the knitter's sewing needle with the tail of yarn left on top of the hat crown and stitch the bobble to it with several stab stitches going right through the bobble.

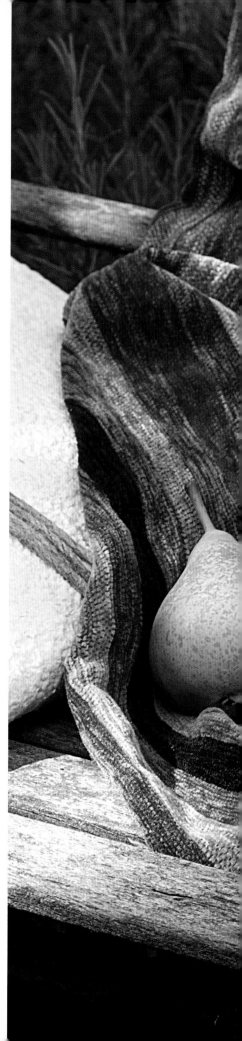

Hip hop cap

A funky, street-style cap that'll put a spring in your step and add flair to an everyday outfit. It's a more complex knitting pattern, but follow the instructions carefully and you'll be proud of the result.

YOU WILL NEED

- One 3½ oz (100 g) ball of Rowan Scottish Tweed Aran in red
- US 11 (8 mm) and US 10½ (7 mm) 24 in (60 cm) circular needles
- Knitter's sewing needle
- Sewing needle and thread

TECHNIQUES

- Knitting for felting, page 110.
- Felting knitting in the washing machine, page 111.
- Drying a felted item, page 111.

Finished size to fit medium and large adult heads.

Abbreviations page 125.

To make
Peak

Both sizes

Using US 11 (8 mm) needle, loosely cast on 34 sts.
Working back and forth, knit 4 rows garter stitch.
Row 5 (RS): Ssk, k to last 2 sts, k2tog. (32 sts)
Row 6: K2tog, k to last 2 sts, ssk. (30 sts)
Rep rows 5–6 until 4 sts remain.
Place rem 4 sts on a holder.
Pick up 8 sts from the peak immediately before the 4 sts on the holder, pick up the 4 sts on the holder, then pick up 8 more sts from the peak.
Place all 20 sts on a holder.

Cap

Using US 10½ (7 mm) needle, cast on 54(60) sts.
Work back and forth.
Row 1: [K1, p1] rep to end, working sts as tightly as possible.
Rep row 1 once more.
Row 3: K5, k2tog, k to last st, sl1, do not turn. (53:59 sts)
Row 4: Knit first st of peak from holder, pass last slipped st of cap over this st, k18 sts from holder, slip last st on holder onto needle. (72:78 sts)
Join into the round, placing marker at round end and being careful not to twist stitches.
Next round: [K1, M1, k2] rep to end. (96:104 sts)
Knit 24 rounds.
Place marker at center stitch.
Next round: [K10(11), k2tog] rep to center marker, [ssk, k10(11)] rep to end.
Knit 2 rounds.
Next round: [K9(10), k2tog] rep to center marker, [ssk, k9(10)] rep to end.
Knit 2 rounds.
Next round: [K8(9), k2tog] rep to center marker, [ssk, k8(9)] rep to end.
Knit 2 rounds.
Cont in patt as set until 8 sts remain.
Next round: [Sl1, k2tog, psso] rep once more, k2tog. (3 sts)
Cut yarn leaving 6 in (15cm) tail. Thread knitter's sewing needle with yarn tail, thread through rem 3 sts and pull up tight. Make a couple of stitches on the inside of the hat to secure the knitting.

Trimming

Using the thumb method and working over both ends of US 10½ (7 mm) needle held together, cast on 17 sts. (This achieves a very loose cast on.)
Slip one end of the needle out of the cast on sts.
Work back and forth.
Row 1: Work into front, back and front of every st, thus making 3 sts from every 1 st cast on. (51 sts)
Bind off very loosely purlwise.

Making up

Weave in any loose ends.

Felting

Curl the trimming up and fasten it with a safety pin to stop it tangling. Following the instructions for Felting Knitting in the Washing Machine, machine-wash the hat to felt it. When the felting process is complete, follow the instructions for Drying a Felted Item.

Finishing

Fold the trimming in half and, using the sewing needle and thread, sew the middle to the top of the crown of the cap.

Classic beret

Based on a traditional pattern, this beret is very simple to knit and make up. Wear it with casual clothes, a chic suit, or a pretty dress— it's so versatile it'll go beautifully with any outfit.

YOU WILL NEED

- One 1¾ oz (50 g) ball of Garnstudio Tomos in pink
- US 10½ (7 mm) 32 in (80 cm) circular needle
- Knitter's sewing needle
- Piece of narrow elastic stretched to fit comfortably around your head and with the ends sewn together to make a circle.
- Decorative button
- Sewing needle and thread

TECHNIQUES

- Knitting for felting, page 110.
- Felting knitting in the washing machine, page 111.
- Drying a felted item, page 111.

Finished size to fit an average adult head.

Abbreviations page 125.

To make
Beret

Loosely cast on 78 sts.
Place marker at round end. Join into the round, being careful not to twist stitches.
Round 1: Purl.
Rep this round seven more times.
Fold the knitted fabric in half, purl-side facing, and place the elastic in the fold. Pick up the first cast on loop and knit it together with the first st on the needle. Repeat with all following cast on loops and matching stitches to make a closed casing for the elastic.

Shape beret
Round 9: [K1, inc in next 2 sts] rep to end. (130 sts)
Knit 25 rounds.

Shape top
Next round: [K11, k2tog] rep to end. (120 sts)
Next round and every alt round: Knit.
Next round: [K10, k2tog] rep to end. (110 sts)
Next round: [K9, k2tog] rep to end. (100 sts)
Next round: [K8, k2tog] rep to end. (90 sts)
Next round: [K7, k2tog] rep to end. (80 sts)
Next round: [K6, k2tog] rep to end. (70 sts)
Knit 2 rounds.
Cut yarn leaving 6 in (15 cm) tail.
Thread knitter's sewing needle with yarn tail, thread through rem sts and pull up tight. Make a few stitches on the inside of the hat to secure the knitting.

Making up

Weave in any loose ends.

Felting

Following the instructions for Felting Knitting in the Washing Machine, machine-wash the hat to felt it. When the felting process is complete, follow the instructions for Drying a Felted Item.

Finishing

Using the sewing needle and thread, sew the decorative button to the top of the beret, covering the gathered center.

Retro pillbox hat

This fabulous little hat is so simple to make and easy to wear. Decorate your hat with one of the felted trimmings shown here, or customize it with beads, bows, or ribbons to make a personal version.

YOU WILL NEED

- One 1¾ oz (50 g) ball of Twilley Freedom in each of black (A) and cream (B)
- US 11 (8 mm) and US 10 (6 mm) 24 in (60 cm) circular needles
- Knitter's sewing needle
- Sewing needle and thread

TECHNIQUES

- Knitting for felting, page 110.
- Felting knitting in the washing machine, page 111.
- Drying a felted item, page 111.
- Felted yarn bobbles, page 114.

Finished size to fit an average adult head.

Abbreviations page 125.

To make
Hat

Sides

Using US 11 (8 mm) needle and A, loosely cast on 16 sts.
Working back and forth, work 120 rows st st. Bind off loosely.

Lower edging

With side piece right-side facing, and using US 10 (6 mm) needle and A, pick up 82 sts (about 2 stitches for every 3 rows) along one (bottom) row edge.
**Starting with a purl row and working back and forth, work 6 rows st st.

Bind off loosely.
Cut yarn leaving a long tail. Thread the knitter's sewing needle with tail and sew the bound off edge of the edging to the back of the row it was picked up from, creating a roll of knitted fabric along the edge of the hat side piece.**

Upper edging

With side piece right-side facing, and using US 10 (6 mm) needle and A, pick up 82 sts along the other (top) row edge.
Rep from ** to **.

Crown

Using US 11 (8 mm) needle and B, pick up 82 sts along the second row of the upper edging. Work back and forth.
Row 1 (WS): Purl.
Row 2: [K7, k2tog, place marker] rep to last st, k1. (73 sts)
Row 3: Purl.
Row 4: [K to 2 sts before marker, k2tog] rep to last st, k1. (64 sts)
Row 5: Purl.
Rep last 2 rows until 19 sts remain.
Next row (RS): [K2tog, remove marker] rep to last st, k1. (10 sts)
Cut yarn leaving a long tail. Thread knitter's sewing needle with the tail, thread through rem 10 sts and pull up tight. Using mattress stitch, sew open sides of crown together. Thread needle with A and sew sides together.

Trimming

Cut 4 10-in (25-cm) lengths of black yarn and 12 10-in (25-cm) lengths of cream yarn.
Lay out half the cream strands, lay the black strands on top, then cover them with the cream strands, so that the black strands are entirely surrounded with cream yarn.
Following the instructions for Beautiful Blue Bracelet (see page 45), soap and rub the bundle of yarn until it forms a solid rod.

Making

Weave in any loose ends on the hat.

Felting

Following the instructions for Felting Knitting in the Washing Machine, machine-wash the hat to felt it. When the felting process is complete, follow the instructions for Drying a Felted Item.

Finishing

Cut slices of the rod of trimming and, using the sewing needle and thread, sew them to the front of the hat, following the photograph for position.

Variation

This pillbox hat is trimmed with a ring of jaunty felt bobbles. Make them following the instructions for Felted Yarn Bobbles and sew them onto the hat after felting it. The yarns used for this hat are:

- One 1¾ oz (50 g) ball of Garnstudio Eskimo in each of pale blue and white/camel/blue.

6
Techniques

Making felt

If you look at wool fibers (fleece fibers or yarn fibers), under a microscope, you can see that each strand is a shaft of overlapping scales. In warm water these scales lift away from the shaft and slip around. Add a little soap and the scales lift and *move even more. As you (or the washing machine) agitate the fibers, the scales crinkle up and attach themselves to their neighbors. The fibers are pulled tightly together, so the fabric shrinks and becomes denser, thereby creating felt. It really is that simple!*

Tools and materials

You need only the most basic equipment to start felting, and all of it is readily available from good craft shops or through the Internet (see Suppliers, page 126).

Fine mesh fabric
Fine mesh fabric for soaping the fibers through.

Bubblewrap
Bubblewrap to lay under the felt while you are working.

Lint-free bath towel
Use an old, lint-free bath towel to cover your work surface.

Bamboo mat
Lay a bamboo mat under the felt while you are working. The mats used in making sushi are ideal.

Plastic
Thick, flexible plastic is used for cutting resist templates from; the material used as underlay for laminate flooring works perfectly. See page 116 for how to use a resist.

Foam
A piece of thick foam is used to dry-felt onto.

Dry felting needle
A dry felting needle is used to add dry wool fibers to a felted item.

Yarn
If you are going to felt knitted fabric, then you'll need a selection of yarns. Each project tells you what to buy.

Soap

If you're felting with fibers or hand-felting knitted fabric, then you'll also need soap. Two kinds are used: a soap that dissolves in water for sprinkling onto the felt and a block of soap for rubbing onto the felt. To make your own soluble soap, half fill a plastic jug with pure soap flakes (the kind sold for hand-washing woolen garments is ideal). Top up the jug with hot water and stir well until all the flakes are dissolved. Leave the mix to stand until it becomes a jelly. To use the soap, just put 1 dessertspoonful into your sprinkler bottle (see below) and add 1 pint of hot water. Shake well to dissolve the soap.

Sprinkling felt with soapy water is simple with your own sprinkler bottle. Take an empty fabric conditioner bottle (the type with a built-in handle is easiest to use) and pierce a few holes in the lid with a skewer. It's as easy as that.

Any bar of pure soap can be used for rubbing. I like to use an olive oil soap as it moisturizes my hands as well as producing a lovely foamy lather for felting.

Wool
Use wool fibers in your choice of colors if you are going to do a fiber-felting project.

Silk
Silk fibers can be mixed in with the wool fibers for a luxuriously soft feel and delicate sheen.

Felting knitted fabric

Felting is a wonderful way of adding a new dimension to knitting. The resulting fabric has a completely different look and feel to knitted fabric. The knitting patterns in this book are simple, so novice knitters will be able to tackle most of them. In fact, if you are a beginner, then felting can be a marvellous tool: it shrinks and smoothes all the stitches together, hiding uneven knitting and covering up minor mistakes.

Knitting for felting

Knitting up a project that is to be felted is not very different to working a conventional knitting project. There are just a few things to bear in mind to help make your felting project successful.

The yarns I have chosen for the knitting projects in this book have been selected for their particular qualities. They usually have high wool content, as it is this fiber that shrinks and becomes felt. As the yarn needs to be washed to felt it, it must not lose too much color or pill too badly. Some yarns will fade a little in the felting process, but this can be an attractive feature. White wool is very hard to felt as it has usually been bleached and this affects its felting properties: I prefer to avoid it completely.

If you are going to substitute a different yarn for the one specified in a project, be sure to match the fiber content or the end result may be quite different to the original. You also need to ensure that you buy the same yardage of yarn or you may not have enough to complete the project: don't rely on the weight of the ball of yarn, check the yardage given on the ball band. You will find a list of all the yarns used in this book, along with their fiber content and yardage, on page 124.

Before you make up a project in a substitute yarn, knit a swatch and felt it to ensure that you like the resulting fabric. Keep a record of each swatched piece, noting the length of time it was washed for to achieve the felted result, and any color fading or pilling. You can quickly build up a library of swatches that will be invaluable in choosing yarns for other felting projects.

Yarns with lower wool content will felt to varying degrees, depending on the amount of wool fiber they contain. Yarns entirely composed of man-made fibers will not felt, but can be knitted in with wool yarns to add color and texture to the item. As the wool yarn shrinks, the man-made yarn will wrinkle up or create little loops that

can give a felted piece a really interesting look.

You will notice that no gauge counts are given on any of the knitted projects in this book. This is because gauge really doesn't affect the end result much at all. Felting projects are usually knitted on larger needles than the ball band suggests, so you won't be able to match the ball band gauge. If you are a particularly tight or loose knitter and are worried about how the felted fabric will look, knit a swatch and felt it to check the end result.

Generally, cast on and bind off loosely to avoid tight edges on a project. If you are making a hat, you can help counteract the tendency the bound-off edge has to roll up by binding off purlwise if the knit side is facing you, and vice versa.

Don't be worried by the appearance of the knitting once you have finished it. It will be enormous and baggy-looking, as you can see in the picture, below left, of the Striped Satchel (page 18) before it was felted. The felting process will shrink and tighten the knitting and all will be well, as the "after felting" picture, below right, shows.

Felting knitting in the washing machine

This is such a simple way of felting a piece of knitting; all the hard work is done for you by the washing machine.

Put the item to be felted in a mesh laundry bag to help prevent loose fibers clogging up the filter on the washing machine. (If you do a lot of felting, you should clean the filter out frequently. Some committed felters even have a separate washing machine that they only use for felting.) If it's a long, narrow item, such as a bag strap, fold it up, and secure it with a safety pin to stop it tangling. Put an old, lint-free towel in the laundry bag along with the item to help agitate the fibers. Add a small amount of liquid fabric detergent and set the machine to a 60° wash.

The trick with felting is knowing when to stop; too soon and the fabric is not fully felted, too late and the fabric is too thick and stiff, and has shrunk so much that the piece is tiny. I check the machine every five minutes or so, peering through the door to see what the piece looks like. As soon as the knitted stitches are no longer visible and the surface of the fabric looks like commercial felt, I stop the machine and spin the water out of it. If you can't see the item well enough through the door, then stop the washing cycle, spin the water out and check the item. If it isn't sufficiently felted, start the cycle again, but do not add any more detergent.

Once the felting process is complete, take the item out of the machine. Rinse it thoroughly in cool water and either spin it gently in the machine or roll it up tightly in a towel and squeeze it to remove excess water.

Drying a felted item

The felt fabric will dry in the shape you mold it into, within reason, so spend some time at this stage to achieve a good result.

Shape the wet item with your hands, pulling and squeezing it into the desired form. The felt is quite pliable, so be careful not to pull it out of shape.

If the item is flat, like a scarf, then lay it out flat on a towel and leave it to dry completely.

To shape a bag, the best thing is to place something of a suitable size and shape (you'll find advice on this with each project), inside it and then leave it to dry. Whatever you put in the bag should be a fairly tight fit so that the felt is slightly stretched around it.

My preferred way of drying a hat is on my head. I put it on, then shape it looking in a mirror and wear it for the day until it is dry. This ensures that it is a perfect fit. If you prefer not to do this, then shape it on something the same circumference as your head and leave it to dry.

Pumps can be left on the foot last to dry, or you can put them on your feet and wear them watching television for the evening so that they dry to fit your feet perfectly.

If you don't like the shape of an item once it has dried don't worry, you can reshape it. Soak the item in warm water, roll it tightly in a towel to soak up excess water, and then just shape it again. However, do remember that you can't make something smaller in the reshaping process.

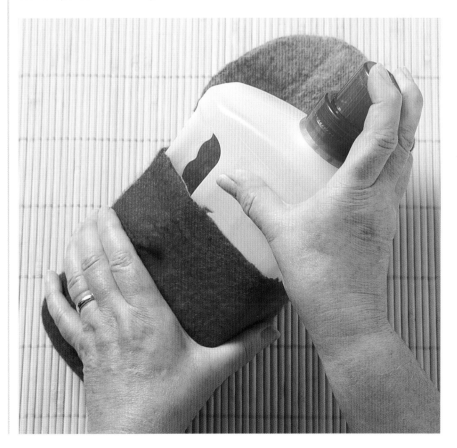

Felting knitting by hand

If you are worried about stopping the felting process in time in the washing machine, you can felt knitting by hand. This method is great for felting more delicate knitted items, such as the Knitted Mesh Scarf (below and page 60). You can also complete the felting process on a fiber-felt project by hand, as shown opposite.

If the item is flat, like a scarf, then use the following method.

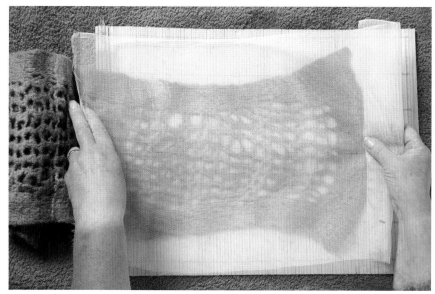

1 Lay a towel out flat and lay a bamboo mat on top of it. Lay the item to be felted flat on the mat. (If it's a long scarf, roll it up to the left of you as shown, and felt a section at a time. As you felt sections, pull them across the worksurface and roll the scarf up on the other side.) Lay a piece of fine mesh fabric over the knitting.

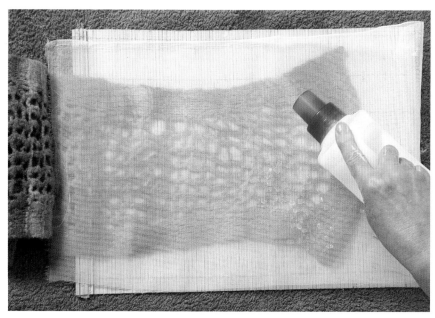

2 Sprinkle warm soapy water from your bottle all over the knitting, making sure it is completely soaked.

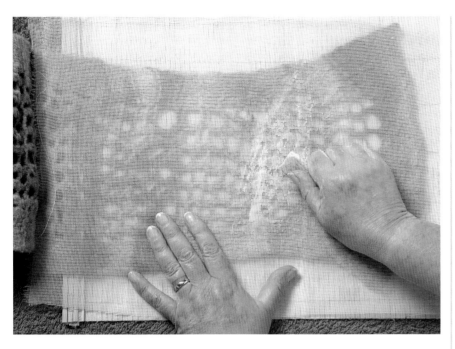

3 Rub a bar of soap over the mesh to push yet more soap into the knitted fabric. Work over a small section of fibers at a time.

4 Using both hands, rub the knitted fabric through the mesh. Rub quite firmly, creating a thick lather that will rub back into the fibers as you work. Continue rubbing for about 15 minutes, then lift up the mesh and check that the fibers have felted together: the knitted stitches should have almost completely disappeared and the fabric surface should look like felt. If the fabric is not sufficiently felted, replace the mesh and rub again for 10 minutes. Rinse the felted item thoroughly in cool water and roll it up tightly in a towel to absorb excess water.

If the item is three-dimensional, like a hat, then hand felt it using this method, which can be used on knitted projects or to finish fiber-felt projects, as shown. Plunge the item into warm soapy water. Agitate it in the water until it is thoroughly soaked.

1 Rub a bar of soap all over the outside of the item.

2 Rub the item with your hands for about 30 minutes. If it hasn't felted to your satisfaction, then add more soap and keep rubbing until you are happy with the item's appearance and size. Remember that you can felt one area more than another just by rubbing it more. This can be an interesting way of altering the size and shape of an item, but if this isn't your intention, then try to rub it evenly all over. Rinse the felt thoroughly in cool water, trying not to rub it any more, and gently squeeze out excess water.

I-cords

I use these simple knitted cords quite a lot to make handles and trimmings for bags, such as the Summer Bag (below and page 20). They are worked on double-pointed needles, and the appropriate needle size and number of stitches needed are given with each project.

Cast on required number of stitches.
Row 1: Knit.
Next row: *Slide the stitches along the right-hand needle so that they are at the right-hand end and the working yarn is at the left of the work. Holding this needle in your left hand, stretch the yarn across the back of the work and knit the first stitch, the one closest to the point of the needle. Pull the working yarn tight and knit the remaining 4 stitches. Repeat from * until the I-cord is the required length.

Felted yarn bobbles

Bobbles can be used as beads and strung together to make jewelry, such as the Pink Bobble Necklace (page 34). They also make fun trimmings and can be used to embellish all sorts of felted pieces. Make bobbles as large or small as you wish by winding the yarn more or less times around more or less fingers.

1 To make a large bobble, wind a pure wool yarn approximately 50 times around two fingers.

2 Slip the bundle of yarn off your fingers and wind more yarn round it. Keep the yarn quite loose, don't pull it tight in the middle.

3 Now turn the bundle through 90 degrees and wind more yarn around it. Again, don't pull the yarn tight.

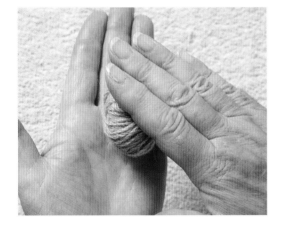

4 Turn the bundle at an angle and wind on more yarn to round off the corners. Make the bundle as close to a ball shape as you can.

5 Roll the bundle of yarn gently between your hands to make it as round as possible.

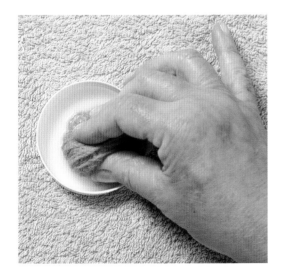

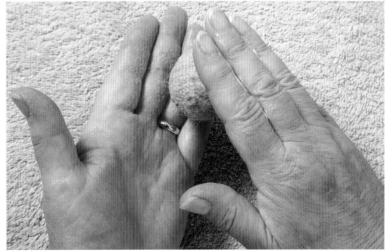

6 Pour a little warm soapy water into a small dish. Dip the ball of yarn into it, pressing it down and turning it to make sure that it's soaked all the way through.

7 Roll the wet ball of yarn between your hands, gently at first and increasing the pressure as the yarn starts to felt together and the ball becomes firmer. About 5–10 minutes of rolling should make a lovely felt bobble.

Felting with fibers

Pure wool fibers of different types, such as merino or alpaca, can also be used to make fabulous felt. The fibers are lovely and soft to the touch, so working with them is a real pleasure. There are two basic methods. Felting Over a Resist, opposite, is used to make projects such as the Pretty Felt Pumps (below and page 74). Felting on Fabric (page 119), is used to create gorgeous scarves, such as the Soft Chiffon Stole (page 56).

Felting over a resist

This involves covering a plastic resist with felted fibers, then removing the resist to create a hollow shape that can be turned quickly and easily into a bag or pair of pretty pumps.

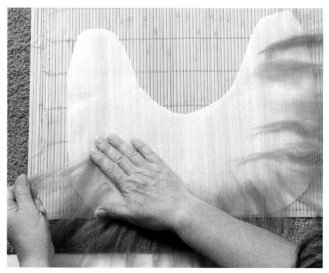

1 Lay a towel flat on your work surface and lay a bamboo mat on top of it. Lay the plastic resist flat on the mat. Pull off small amounts of fiber and start by laying them around the edges of the resist, making sure they overlap the edges by about half their length.

2 Continue pulling off and laying down small amounts of fiber to cover the whole resist with a single layer of fiber.

3 Now cover the resist with a second layer of fibers placed at right angles to the first layer as far as possible. Again, make sure that you overlap the edges. Here, the second layer is a different color to the first layer, so the inside of the hollow shape will be a different color to the outside.

4 Carefully lay a piece of mesh fabric over the whole shape without disturbing any fibers. Sprinkle hot soapy water over the mesh, making sure that the fibers lying on the resist are soaked, but keeping the fibers that overlap the edges as dry as possible.

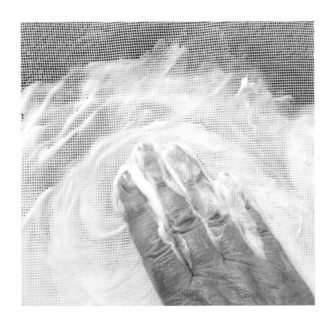

5 Gently at first, rub the fibers through the mesh using your fingers. Keep rubbing to create a lather that is rubbed back into the fibers. After rubbing for about 15–20 minutes, carefully lift off the mesh to check that the fibers have felted together into a solid fabric. If they haven't, replace the mesh and rub again.

6 Lift off the mesh and set it aside. Carefully turn the resist over, making sure that the felt doesn't slide off. Flip the fibers overlapping the edges of the resist over onto the side now facing you. Smooth them down onto the plastic, if necessary, sprinkling on a little water to make them lie flat.

Repeat Steps 1–6 on the side of the plastic resist now facing you. When you reach Step 6, smooth the overlapping fibers down onto the existing felt so that they blend into it. Leave the felt to dry.

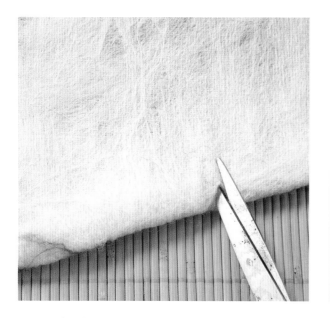

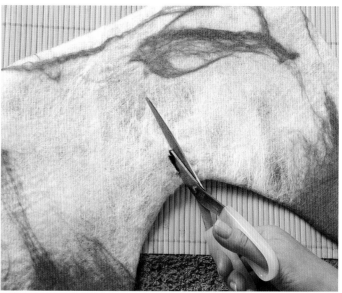

7 Decide where you want to cut the felt according to the project you are making. Using a pair of sharp-pointed scissors, carefully snip into one layer of the felt, right at the edge. Be sure not to cut through the plastic or bottom layer of felt.

8 Cut right across the top layer, then, if required, turn the felt over and cut through the other layer.

9 Slide the resist out of the middle of the felt, being careful not to pull the felt out of shape.

Felting on fabric

This method of felting, also known as nuno felting, involves melding a thin layer of wool fibers with a fine cloth, such as silk chiffon, to create a gorgeous fabric that drapes beautifully and is wonderfully textural.

1 Lay a towel flat on your work surface and lay the piece of fabric out on top of it. Arrange a thin layer of wool fibers on top of the fabric. You can cover almost the whole surface, as shown here, or arrange the fibers in a simple pattern. Do be aware that the slightest breeze can blow the fine fibers away, so don't sneeze at this stage!

2 Carefully lay a piece of mesh fabric over the fibers without disturbing any of them. Sprinkle warm soapy water over the mesh, making sure that all the fibers are soaked.

3 Very gently, rub a bar of soap over a small section of fibers at a time. Then, with your fingers, rub the soaped area to create a lather that is rubbed back into the fibers. Rub each area for about 10–15 minutes.

Once you have soaped and rubbed all the cloth, very carefully lift off the mesh. Gently run your fingers over the felted surface to check that the fibers and cloth are melded together. If any areas are loose, replace the mesh and rub them again. Leave the finished fabric to dry.

Templates

This sample template shows you how your template for the
Pretty Felt Pumps (page 74 and opposite) should look.

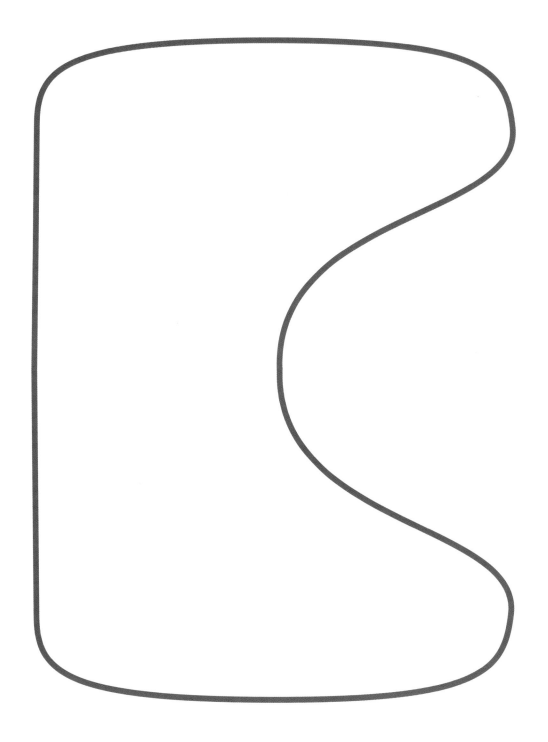

Above is the template for the **Pink Flower Bag** (page 14 and opposite). Enlarge this to the size you want the bag to be, plus 30 per cent.

Below is the template for the **Silky Shoe Bag** (page 22). Enlarge this to the size you want the bag to be, plus 30 per cent.

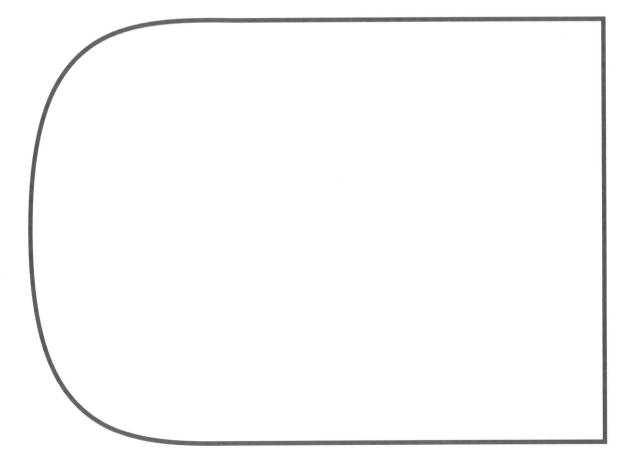

Yarn information

Adriafil Baba
1¾ oz (50 g)
100% merino wool
66 yd (60 m)

Anny Blatt Fleur
1¾ oz (50 g)
92% wool, 8% polyamide
61 yd (56 m)

Anny Blatt Vega
1¾ oz (50 g)
55% wool, 45% nylon
44 yd (40 m)

Cascade 220
3½ oz (100 g)
100% wool
220 yd (201 m)

Colinette Giotto
1¾ oz (50 g)
50% cotton, 40% rayon, 10% nylon
157 yd (144 m)

Colinette Point 5
3½ oz (100 g)
100% wool
54 yd (50 m)

Debbie Bliss Maya
3½ oz (100 g)
100% wool
137 yd (126 m)

Felt Studio Falkland Wool Siri
1¾ oz (50 g)
100% wool
54 yd (50 m)

Garnstudio Eskimo
1¾ oz (50 g)
100% wool
54 yd (50 m)

Karabella Roses
1 oz (25 g)
100% merino
197 yd (180 m)

Knitting4fun Chunky
3½ oz (100 g)
100% wool
109 yd (100 m)

Kollage Illumination
1¾ oz (50 g)
mohair, viscose, polyamide mix
100 yd (91.4 m)

Noro Kureyon
1¾ oz (50 g)
100% wool
100 yd (91.4 m)

Peace Fleece Russian American
3½ oz (100 g)
100% wool
109 yd (100 m)

Plymouth Spazzini
1¾ oz (50 g)
75% wool, 25% nylon
75 yd (68.5 m)

Prism Impressions
1¾ oz (50 g)
rayon, cotton, mohair, kid mohair,
nylon, wool, silk, alpaca, and poly mix
150 yd (137 m)

Rooster Almerino Aran
1¾ oz (50 g)
50% alpaca, 50% merino
103 yd (94 m)

Rooster Almerino DK
1¾ oz (50 g)
50% alpaca, 50% merino
123 yd (112.5 m)

Rowan Scottish Tweed Aran
3½ oz (100 g)
100% wool
186 yd (170 m)

Tahki Poppy
1¾ oz (50 g)
20% cotton, 27% acrylic, 45% nylon
81 yd (74 m)

Texere Alpaca Select
1¾ oz (50 g)
100% alpaca
115 yd (105 m)

Twilley Chic
1¾ oz (50 g)
60% nylon, 30% polyester, 10%
metalized polyester
44 yd (40 m)

Twilley Freedom
1¾ oz (50 g)
100% wool
120 yd (110 m)

Twilley Frizzante
1¾ oz (50 g)
58% nylon, 30% rayon, 12% acrylic
60 yd (55 m)

Twilley Paris Mohair
1¾ oz (50 g)
81% mohair, 11% wool, 8% nylon
109 yd (100 m)

Twilley Spirit
1¾ oz (50 g)
100% wool
55 yd (50 m)

Victoria Smedley MoBair Hand-dyed Alpaca Wool Bouclé
Approx 1¾ oz (50 g)
Alpaca, wool mix
Yd/m varies

Wendy Roxy
1¾ oz (50 g)
55% wool, 30% rayon, 11% polyester
60 yd (55 m)

Abbreviations

( )   contain metric conversions and needle sizes, stitch counts, and larger pattern sizes where appropriate.

[ ]   follow instructions within brackets the number of times stated after the brackets.

* *   follow instructions between asterisks the number of times stated after the last asterisk.

ABC etc colors as indicated in the knitting pattern.

approx approximately

alt   alternate

beg   beginning

cm   centimeter(s)

cont   continue

foll   following

folls   follows

g   grams

in   inch(es)

inc   increase. Knit into the front and then the back of a stitch to make one extra stitch.

k   knit

k2tog   knit the next two stitches together. Put the right-hand needle knitwise through the next two stitches and knit them together to make them into one stitch.

m   metre(s)

mm   millimetres

M1   make one stitch. From the front, put the tip of the left-hand needle under the strand of yarn lying between the last stitch worked and the next one. Lift the strand up and knit into the back of it to make one extra stitch.

oz   ounces

p   purl

p2tog   purl the next two stitches together. Put the right-hand needle purlwise through the next two stitches and purl them together to make them into one stitch.

patt   pattern

psso   pass slipped stitch over. Pass the stitch that has been slipped over the next stitch to the left on the needle.

rem   remaining

rep   repeat

RS   right side of the work.

sl   slip

ssk   slip, slip, knit. One at a time, slip the next two stitches knitwise onto the right-hand needle. Put the left-hand needle through the stitches, in front of the right-hand needle, and knit the two stitches together to make them into one stitch.

ssp   slip, slip, purl. One at a time, slip the next two stitches purlwise onto the right-hand needle. Put the left-hand needle through the stitches, behind the right-hand needle, and purl the two stitches together to make them into one stitch.

st st   stocking stitch

st(s)   stitch(es)

WS   wrong side of the work.

yd   yard(s)

yo   yarn over. Wrap the yarn around the needle counterclockwise, finishing with it in position to work the next stitch.

US/UK terms

stockinette stitch	stocking stitch
bind off	cast off
gauge	tension

Knitting needle conversions

US	Metric	Old UK
0	2 mm	14
1	2.25 mm	13
	2.50 mm	
2	2.75 mm	12
	3 mm	11
3	3.25 mm	10
4	3.50 mm	
5	3.75 mm	9
6	4 mm	8
7	4.50 mm	7
8	5 mm	6
9	5.5 mm	5
10	6 mm	4
10½	6.5 mm	3
	7 mm	2
	7.5 mm	1
11	8 mm	0
13	9 mm	00
15	10 mm	000
19	15 mm	
35	19 mm	
50	25 mm	

Measurements

All measurements are given in imperial and metric. While every effort has been made to ensure consistency, you should choose one system only to work in.

Suppliers

Most supplies required for the projects included in this book may be found at your local craft or yarn shop. For specialty products, check the Web sites listed here.

YARNS

Adriafil Yarns
www.adriafil.com for stockists.

Anny Blatt
www.annyblatt.com for stockists.

Cascade Yarns
www.cascadeyarns.com for stockists.

Colinette Yarns
www.colinette.com for stockists.

Debbie Bliss
www.debbieblissonline.com for stockists.

Felt Studio
www.feltstudio.com for stockists.

Garnstudio
www.garnstudio.com for stockists.

Karabella Yarns
www.karabellayarns.com for stockists.

Knitting4fun
www.knitting4fun.com for stockists.

Kollage Yarns
www.kollageyarns.com for stockists.

Noro
www.designeryarns.uk.com for stockists.

Peace Fleece
www.peacefleece.com for stockists.

Plymouth Yarn Co
www.plymouthyarn.com for stockists.

Prism Yarns
www.prismyarn.com for stockists.

Rooster Yarns
www.roosteryarns.com for stockists.

Rowan Yarns
www.knitrowan.com for stockists.

Tahki
www.tahkistacycharles.com for stockists.

Texere Yarns
www.texere.co.uk for stockists.

Twilleys of Stamford
www.twilleys.co.uk for stockists.

Victoria Smedley
www.Victoria@MoBair.co.uk

Wendy Roxy
www.tbramsden.co.uk

FELTING FIBERS

Wingham Wool Work
www.winghamwoolwork.co.uk

HANDLES AND BAG TRIMMINGS

U-handbags
www.u-handbags.com

Bags of Handles
www.bagsofhandles.co.uk

BUTTONS

The Button Company
www.buttoncompany.co.uk

Button Mad
www.buttonmad.com

BEADS

Beads Direct
www.beadsdirect.co.uk

Viking Loom
www.vikingloom.co.uk

Rare Bird
Liz Welch Friendly Plastic Shop
www.rarebird.co.uk

SHOE LASTS

Wingham Wool Work
www.winghamwoolwork.co.uk

WIRE

Scientific Wire
www.wires.co.uk

SILK CHIFFON SCARVES

Marr Haven Wool Farm
www.marrhaven.com

BAMBOO MATS AND RESISTS

Bamboo mats can be bought from any supplier of sushi-making equipment and laminate underlay for resists from home improvement stores.

Acknowledgments

Felt Style, what a journey, creating pieces from landscapes, colors, and plants that have inspired me.

It has been great fun and special thanks must go to Cindy Richards who has again allowed me to turn dreams into reality, and not forgetting all the staff at Cico who work so hard.

Special thanks to the following companies and individuals who have gone the extra mile for me:
Austin and Gabrielle Ramsden at Ramsden's Yarns.
Romy at Viking Loom.
Liz Welsh at Rare Bird.
Lisa at u-handbags.
Maggie Allinson at Bags of Handles.

Kate Haxell, my editor, who has been there every step of the way; thank you, Kate.

Geoff Dann for fun photo sessions and truly great pics.

Kate Strutt for agreeing to model for me; Kate, thank you, it was done with such style.

Thanks also to:
Stylist Sammie Bell; wow, you are so creative, thank you.
Designer Claire Legemah; the book looks fabulous, thank you.
Pattern checker Marilyn Wilson.

My darling husband, Nigel, who is still patient with me, still making me laugh, always calm, and always believing in me, he shares my dreams.

I must also mention my two children, James and Emma, both successful in their own fields, but who still make the journey of life fun and do inspire me. You both amaze me.

My partner and mother-in-law, Cindy, who does everything and a lot of the knitting as well; bless you.

M.J.H., you know who you are.
Thank you for giving me tomorrow,
I will never forget.

To all of you wishing you could, or had, or did—do it.

Take hold of your dream
Catch onto that star
Have faith in yourself
You are what you are.
CHRISSIE DAY.

Index